SOCIAL PHOBIA

SOCIAL PHOBIA

Alleviating Anxiety in an Age of Self-Promotion

Donald Capps

Chalice Press
St. Louis, Missouri

Dedicated to Owe Wikstrom

"The tongue of the wise brings healing."
—Proverbs 12:18

Contents

Acknowledgments

Margarete Ziemer helped me identify and acquire copies of most of the research studies that I discuss here. I deeply appreciate her own research skills and the energy and spirit she brought to an exacting, onerous task. Joan Blyth-Lovell typed the final manuscript with greater efficiency and attention to detail than any author has a right to expect. Jon Berquist, academic editor at Chalice Press, has been a model editor—encouraging, helpful, and efficient (without having to make a great show of it). The book is dedicated to Owe Wikstrom, Professor of Psychology of Religion at Uppsala University. He is the author of many books, an expert on the writings of Feodor Dostoevski, a priest in the Church of Sweden, husband of a dedicated physician, father of more children than I (perhaps even he) can keep track of, and a man of great liberality, good humor, and unstinting kindness.

A late-blooming burgundy hollyhock sways
across the kitchen window in a light breeze
as I draw a tumbler of well-water at the sink.

At dinner I laughed with the rest
but in truth I prefer the sound
of pages turning, and coals shifting
abruptly in the stove. I left before ten
pleading a long drive home.

Why do people give dinner parties? Why did I
say I'd come? I suppose no one there was entirely
at ease. Again the flower leans this way:
You know it's impolite to stare. I'll put
out the light.

—Jane Kenyon

* *From "After the Dinner Party,"* Let Evening
Come. *Saint Paul, Minn., Graywolf Press, 1990.*
Used by permission.

Preface

This is a book about social phobia, a psychological problem that has plagued the lives of a vast number of persons throughout the centuries, but a problem that is perhaps more serious today than ever before because those who are afflicted with it are, as a consequence, ill-equipped to compete in our current age of self-promotion. Unfortunately, most persons who are social phobics are unaware that they are social phobics. They may describe themselves as "introverted," and they may be conscious of the fact that they do not like to socialize or make speeches in front of an audience, but they are unaware that there *is* such a thing as social phobia, that it has been the object of considerable research over the past several decades, and that there are methods for treating it.

This book is primarily intended for readers who may "see" themselves in this book and recognize that they fit the description of a "social phobic." It is also for readers who are immediate relatives of a person who is socially phobic or have close working relationships or friendships with someone who is phobic. This book is also intended for church leaders who may profit from knowing more about social phobia. Researchers note that social phobics are more likely to attend church services than to become involved in more personally demanding social gatherings. This is because churches allow for rather marginal or restrained participation. Thus, church leaders would do well to know that there are significant numbers of social phobics in their congregations, and that their personal, social, and religious needs are not the same as those of non-social phobics. This is not, however, a book on pastoral counseling per se because it is not very likely that a parishioner will seek counseling from a pastor for this problem. Even if she does, this is a problem that ordinarily requires special therapeutic expertise.

I have drawn extensively on the research literature on social phobia in writing this book. Some readers may find this literature to be rather technical, but I have made a conscientious effort to make it accessible to the general reader. I am also aware that social phobics tend to be thoughtful, intelligent persons, and that they do not appreciate being talked down to. Consequently, I have especially wanted to avoid a similar condescension in the writing of this book. Because I operate on the assumption that readers will *not* seek professional treatment for this problem (and that their spouses and friends will be unsuccessful in their efforts to get them to seek professional help), I have devoted several chapters in this book to the treatment methods that have been developed for social phobia in the belief that readers can learn a great deal about how to help themselves by learning how therapists have helped others.

My own interest in the subject of this book derives from the fact that I consider myself to be a "low-grade" (or "subthreshold") social phobic; and, like most persons who have this problem, I have not sought professional treatment for it. I have read a great deal on the subject, however, and have found this reading to be informative and helpful. For reasons that will become clear to the reader of this book, I do not expect to become "cured" of this problem. In fact, even if there were a "cure" for it, I would think long and hard before taking it, for cures also have their costs. In any event, this does not seem to be a decision for me (or for anyone else who is socially phobic) to make, for there seems to be no lasting cure for social phobia, only some valuable remedies to make it more tolerable. These remedies are thoroughly discussed in the pages to follow.

My reason for writing this book is not, however, so that I might engage in personal confession, thus experiencing a kind of catharsis. In fact, as the reader will also discover from reading this book (if he is not already aware of it), the social phobic does not like to make himself the center of attention. Social phobics are therefore unlikely to write a book about their personal struggles, to appear on talk shows, or even to want to talk to family members or intimate friends about their problem. One practical reason for this is that they are especially aware—almost to a paranoidal degree—that their phobia will be held against them in terms of employment opportunities, career advancement, and the making and keeping of friends. Given the very nature of the problem, efforts to organize social phobia support groups are usually unsuccessful.

Thus, I have written this book for other reasons. One is that very little has been written on social phobia for the general reader. The few books that are available on the subject have been written for the trained professional. This is especially regrettable in the case of social phobia because, as indicated, only a small percentage of persons with this affliction seek professional treatment for it. My own experience, however, tells me that one can be helped by reading about social phobia, much in the same way, perhaps, that one who suffers from a physical disability is helped by reading about its characteristics, how it will affect her life, and how others have coped with it.

My second reason for writing this book is that social phobia has some very important implications for religion. While this could be said of virtually any psychological disorder or problem, social phobia has special significance for religion *today* because it unwittingly represents a protest against the reigning spirit of our age. If ours is an age of self-promotion, an age in which one must promote oneself in order to "get ahead" and achieve "influence" and "power," then social phobia is a quiet but stubborn protest against the age in which we live. In its own unassuming and subversive way, it is *prophetic;* not, however, in the sense that our age tends to understand the prophetic—as "speaking out" against injustice—but in the sense of a quiet, persistent refusal to give those who are dominant in our society the deference that they seek but rarely deserve or merit. For this reason, a "cure" for social phobia, if one existed, might make one feel more comfortable in a world that is, in many respects, inimical to fundamental Christian views regarding self-aggrandizing attitudes and behavior. As "prophetic," social phobics may not be able to envision a time when justice will prevail, but they can exemplify—for themselves and others—the liberating freedom that comes from accepting—and embracing—their *inability* to achieve the influence and power to which others *can* aspire.

Introduction

"I've suffered from severe anxiety since as far back as I can remember. Grammar school and high school were absolute torture for me. Even though I did my homework, studied, and knew the answers most of the time, I spent the whole day, every single day for twelve long years, living in mortal fear and dread of being called on and singled out by the teacher. If I was called on, I froze with panic and anxiety to the extent my mind literally went blank. I couldn't think or give an answer even if a gun had been pointed at my head."

"I am a twenty-four-year-old secretary who would love to get married and have children. However, I blush in any situation where a man expresses the least bit of interest. Even a 'hello' can put me in a state of panic. As a result, I cannot date. Although men apparently find me attractive, this is a mixed blessing. On the one hand, I feel good about myself and think something positive might happen. On the other hand, I'm extremely self-conscious knowing that men may be looking at me. As a result, I've actually changed my hair (in a negative way) or purposely worn unattractive clothes so that people (mainly men) will not notice me. Work is also impossible! I want to do an excellent job, but not so good that I'll elicit some type of attention. I once quit a job, one in which I was extremely happy, because the firm was going to give me an award for outstanding performance at a dinner banquet. I missed the dinner, pretending to be ill, but that only made matters worse. Then they invited me to a smaller 'get-together' in my honor. That was it. I just left on Friday afternoon without notice."

"I am a thirty-seven-year-old basic research scientist and I cannot attend any meetings or give presentations out of fear of having a panic attack. I only have these bouts of terror in situations that elicit scrutiny from other people in either scientific or social situations. Although I have always been introspective, this only started becoming a major problem during the past two years (after publishing a series of findings recognized as a major advance in my field). The combined effects of increased recognition and social self-consciousness are destroying my life."

"I have been unable to eat in public. I have always believed that phobias are, in part, a manifestation of stress but triggered by particular events. In my case, throughout my childhood and as an early adult, my father, who had polio, was subject to severe choking episodes when he ate. These episodes were extremely frightening for me to witness and certainly made me sensitive to the possibility of choking. I did not have trouble eating, however, until becoming an adult, first for a short period in my twenties and now, much more severely for the past two years."

"I have a fear of writing in public. It began four or five years ago when I would occasionally become extremely anxious at the prospect of signing any sort of 'official' form in front of others. Since these incidents were rather sporadic, I was able to rationalize them away by thinking, 'I haven't had lunch yet, so I'm a little shaky,' or 'Anybody would be nervous signing a bank application,' etc. However, about six months ago I had an 'attack' at a gas station while attempting to sign a credit card slip. My hands became so weak and shaky I was unable to hold a pen, let alone sign my name. Since that experience, I have avoided any situation where signing or writing might even be a remote possibility."

"I have suffered from being unable to urinate in front of other men since before high school. It has been the most frustrating reality of my life. The problem became so acute in college dorm-living that I contemplated suicide at that time. I am now fifty-one years of age and still avoid gatherings I should go to but can't bring myself to attend."

What these six persons (from Uhde et al. 1991) have in common is that they suffer from social phobia, an anxiety disorder that causes a great deal of ongoing frustration and significantly reduces a person's overall effectiveness in human interactions. Its major characteristic is the fear of negative evaluation in a social situation. This fear leads a person either to avoid certain social situations or to experience moderate to high levels of anxiety as she endures unavoidable ones. This is a chronic disorder, meaning that it will not suddenly or even gradually disappear with the passage of time. When persons seek treatment for it, many experience only limited improvement. In even the most successful cases some symptoms nearly always remain.

On the other hand, professional treatment is rarely without some benefit, and this raises the perplexing question of why the vast majority of social phobics never seek professional help. Various answers have been put forward: They may not know that treatment is available; they may have reconciled themselves to living with it; or the nature of the disorder makes it difficult for them to seek help, since the very seeking of help places them in a social situation where negative evaluation is anticipated. Also, many social phobics are unaware of the fact that they have this disorder. This often only comes to light when they have sought professional help for another problem, such as alcohol abuse or depression. Moreover, social phobics usually have a long history of having learned to adapt to the problem, which means that they tend not to have an experience, as do persons afflicted with addictive disorders, of "hitting bottom," of being in desperate and urgent need of help. Consequently, the social phobic does not feel intense need at any given moment or juncture in life to get help.

Social phobia is one of three major types of phobia. The other phobias are *specific* phobias, or phobias involving a single feared object or situation (for example, specific animals, snakes, thunderstorms, heights); and *agoraphobia*, the fear of having a panic attack when venturing out into public places (for example, sidewalks, highways, airplanes, shopping malls). In contrast to many specific phobias, the situations that evoke social phobia are difficult to avoid. In comparison to agoraphobia, it is less dramatic but more common. Among the three types of phobia described in the *Diagnostic and Statistical Manual of Mental Disorders*, or *DSM-IV* (1994), it was the last to be identified as a discrete disorder having its own characteristic features and its own preferred treatments. Prior to 1966, when it was identified as a discrete phobia (by Marks and Gelder, 1966), it was listed among the specific phobias. Marks and Gelder identified it as a separate, distinct phobia because it differed from specific phobias and agoraphobia in terms of age of onset. Specific phobias tend to emerge in early to late childhood, and agoraphobia usually emerges in young adulthood (mid-twenties). Social phobia more typically develops in adolescence.

The psychiatric community's tardiness in discovering its distinctiveness and prevalence reflects the fact that social phobia tends to go unnoticed in real life. It receives very little public attention or notice in the media. Also, unlike many of the specific phobias and agoraphobia, social phobia is not very dramatic and not very exciting to study or to treat. Unlike many of the specific phobias, social phobia is complex and for this reason alone is more difficult to treat and less responsive to treatment efforts. Unlike agoraphobia, it lacks the drama that accompanies the agoraphobic's panic attacks. If social phobia is not dramatic, it is, however, challenging to study and treat because of its many paradoxes. For example, while reserved and hesitant in social gatherings, social phobics tend to be affiliative persons. They genuinely want to engage in social situations, and they often choose to do so even when such engagement causes them considerable anxiety. Social phobics should not be confused with antisocial persons who always prefer to be alone. This means that social phobics are to be found in all sorts of social contexts, and the fact that they *are* social phobics may not be obvious or even easily detected. They themselves might be unaware that they fit this category of anxiety disorders.

Another paradox is that social phobics betray few, if any, symptoms of the disorder in family relationships and among close friends, but experience severe anxiety in many other social contexts. Why are they comfortable in some social contexts and not in others? As I discuss in chapter 1, a leading explanation for this anomaly is that social phobics are unusually sensitive to the dominance/submission dynamics in social situations, and these dynamics are more clearly established—and thus predictable—in family relations and with intimate friends.

Yet another paradox is the fact that if social phobics seek professional help, they necessarily place themselves in an anxiety-producing social situation, for the central feature of social phobia is the fear of negative evaluation in a social context, and the whole therapeutic ethos is one in which they, as clients or patients, experience themselves to be at a clear social disadvantage. Thus, the tragedy is that the vast majority of social phobics do not seek professional help even when they are aware that help is available and even when their suffering is severely debilitating. This means that for most persons the disorder is one that they try to learn to live with, doing what they can on their own to minimize its inhibiting and disruptive effects on their daily lives. Because it is a chronic disorder, one that does not disappear in time or go into remission, this means that they have reconciled themselves to living with it for the rest of their lives. Thus, it can be very helpful for social phobics and for persons who are closely related to a social phobic to know something about this disorder. For the social phobic, knowledge about the disorder may provide some comfort and even help in developing better strategies for coping with it. For relatives and friends of a social phobic, knowledge about the disorder may help them to be more understanding and tolerant, especially when he exhibits seemingly inconsistent behavior, such as accepting an invitation to one party while refusing another.

In chapter 1, I discuss social phobia as an anxiety disorder and clarify what it means to say that it involves anxiety and fear. I also discuss the general consensus of clinicians and researchers that social phobia has some basis in innate (or genetic) factors, but that early environmental stress also plays a critical role in determining whether an individual will actually become a social phobic.

In chapter 2, I discuss the diagnostic criteria that are used to determine whether or not a person is afflicted with social phobia. I also address the role played by various demographic factors in the development and maintenance of social phobia, including such key issues as age, gender, socioeconomic class, religious identification, and race. I also cite the few cross-cultural studies that have been conducted to date.

In chapter 3, I identify and discuss the various types of social phobia, explore the protective self-representational style of social phobics, and conclude with a consideration of social phobics' mistrust of social situations.

Chapter 4 centers on the more established (or traditional) methods for treating social phobia, most of which were developed in the treatment of specific phobias and agoraphobia and then adapted to the treatment of social phobics. In chapter 5, I focus on the more recently developed methods, most of which were specifically created for social phobia, giving particular attention to the newer cognitive approaches. In chapter 6 I discuss psychotherapeutic treatment of social phobics, giving particular attention to the psychoanalytic treatment of social phobia. While psychoanalysis is a very traditional method of treatment, the application of psychoanalytic theories and treatment methods to social phobia is a new and developing field. My purpose in discussing these treatment methods in chapters 4 to 6 is not to provide a brief primer on how to counsel social phobics but to identify what has been learned from these treatment methods about social phobia itself. In this way, I make available to the reader useful—and usable—information about how social phobia is understood and treated today.

In chapter 7, I consider social phobia from a transcultural perspective, focusing on Ken-Ichiro Okano's (1994) exploration of the ways in which cultural values in Japan and America influence the meanings assigned to social phobic behavior in these two countries. As it is now well established that cultural meanings and values have considerable impact on how physical and mental disorders are experienced, this discussion will demonstrate that many of the meanings automatically attached to social phobia derive from the culture. Conversely, because social phobia involves an anticipated negative judgment regarding one's behavior in a social situation, social phobia poses a challenge to the very cultural norms and values that are used to define it.

In chapter 8, I explore the role that religion can play in helping to alleviate the anxiety associated with social phobia. This chapter takes its cue from William James' observation, at the turn of the century, that whereas classical religious views of human nature have emphasized the problem of human volition (or will), the more recent, clinically-oriented view (reflected in the mental hygiene movement of his day) emphasizes the problem of fear. While James does not apply this observed shift in emphasis from will to fear specifically to social phobia, I show the relevance of his observation to social phobia. What underlies the social phobic's anxiety is a deep but often unrecognized sense of fear. I also present self-psychologist Heinz Kohut's concepts of the calming structure and the self-object, both of which help to alleviate anxiety, and I suggest that for the social phobic religion may be the source of both.

While it is very unlikely that the social phobic will ever totally overcome her instinctive habit of withdrawing from feared social situations, there is considerable clinical evidence that the fear can be contracted or reduced to more manageable, less anxiety-evoking levels. Also, by becoming more aware of the reasons why he reacts with anxiety in one situation and not another, the social phobic can develop effective strategies for "working around" (or avoiding) situations that are painful or undergone at too great a psychic price.

A final introductory comment: Oskar Pfister, the Swiss pastor who was a lifelong friend of Sigmund Freud, wrote a major book titled *Christianity and Fear* (1948). It was first published in 1944, five years after Freud's death. His basic argument was that the true religious response to fear is love. He made much use of the biblical affirmation that "There is no fear in love, but perfect love casts out fear; for fear has to do with punishment, and whoever fears has not reached perfection in love." (1 John 4:18). He brought psychoanalytic insight to bear on the issue of fear, especially focusing on the compulsions and obsessions resulting from an excessively self-punitive conscience. Simultaneously, he highlighted Jesus' message of love, and noted that Christianity has consistently violated this message by actively promoting fear, usually in the interests of maintaining dogmatic purity. With the exception of a few examples of patients who experienced phobic reactions to specific words and numbers, he gave very little attention to phobia, and none at all to social phobia. Thus, my book is an attempt to relate Pfister's concern with fear to an issue—social phobia—that was not of primary importance to him but is every bit as relevant to the attempt to bring religious resources to bear on a frustrating, evendebilitating, psychosocial problem.

CHAPTER 1

Social Phobia as an Anxiety Disorder

Social phobia has been recognized in medical writings from antiquity. The Greek physician Hippocrates had a patient who "through bashfulness, suspicion, and timorousness, will not be seen abroad; loves darkness as life, and cannot endure the light, or to sit in lightsome places; his hat still in his eyes, he will neither see, nor be seen by his good will. He dare not come in company for fear he should be misused, disgraced, overshoot himself in gestures or speeches, or be sick; he thinks every man observes him" (Greist 1995, 5). In the nineteenth century, the English poet William Cowper tried to hang himself the morning he was scheduled to appear before the House of Lords to be examined for a minor position in the British government. Of this dreadful examination he wrote: "They whose spirits are forced like mine, to whom a public examination of themselves on any occasion is mortal poison, may have some idea of the horrors of my situation; others can have none" (Quinlan 1953, 360). Charles Darwin, in a book on human emotions published in 1872, tells about a small dinner party given in honor of an extremely shy man, who, when he rose to return thanks, repeated the speech that he had learned by heart in absolute silence, not uttering a single word but acting as if he were speaking with much emphasis. His friends, perceiving what was happening, loudly applauded the imaginary bursts of eloquence whenever his gestures indicated a pause, and the man never discovered that he had remained completely silent the whole time. Afterward, he commented to a friend that he thought he had succeeded remarkably well (Darwin 1998, 321).

Not all social phobics lead such impaired lives. Many manage to fashion lives that minimize the anxiety, such as by working at home or

7

taking jobs involving little interpersonal interaction. Yet, in a study of the functional impairment suffered by social phobics (Schneier et al. 1994), it was reported that more than half of the social phobics they studied "reported at least moderate impairment at some time in their lives, due to social anxiety and avoidance, in areas of education, employment, family relationships, marriage/romantic relationships, friendship/social network, and other interests" (322). They "are able to work at a job appropriate to their abilities, but clearly perform beneath their abilities; they have clear impairment in dating activities or minor marital problems; they are able to have a few close friends, but friendships are fewer than desired; and they are able to participate in some non-work interests (e.g., religious activities, clubs, hobbies, sports), but they avoid some activities due to social phobic symptoms." The only aspect of their lives in which they do not suffer functional impairment is in family relationships: "In family functioning and activities of daily living, they experience some distress, but no clear impairment of functioning" (324).

The numbers of persons who are afflicted with social phobia is difficult to determine because few social phobics seek professional treatment. However, according to the *Diagnostic and Statistical Manual (DSM-IV)*, published by The American Psychiatric Association, the mental health profession's "Bible," epidemiological and community-based studies have reported a lifetime prevalence of social phobia ranging from 3 to 13 percent of the American population (414). The reported prevalence varies depending on the threshold used to determine distress or impairment and the number of types of social situations specifically surveyed. In one study, 20 percent reported excessive fear of public speaking and performance but only 2 percent appeared to experience enough impairment or distress to warrant a diagnosis of social phobia (414). In the general population, most individuals with social phobia fear public speaking, whereas somewhat less than half fear speaking to strangers or meeting new people. Other performance fears, such as eating, drinking, or writing in public or using a public restroom, appear to be less common. In clinical settings, the vast majority of persons with social phobia fear more than one type of social situation (414).

Social phobia is rarely the reason for admission to inpatient settings. In outpatient clinics, rates of social phobia have ranged between 10 to 20 percent of individuals with anxiety disorders (the group of disorders with which phobias are classified by *DSM-IV*), but these rates vary widely according to the site (414). Researchers also warn that the wide variety of estimates of social phobia indicate that it is an especially difficult disorder to measure. When they use diagnostic interview schedules to measure social phobia, their agreement among themselves on a given subject is relatively low. One reason for this is that social phobia "can be an easy disorder to conceal from friends and acquaintances. As most people are reluctant to admit to a disability they need not publicize, some may not have admitted it to interviewers" (Reich 1986, 130).

Social phobia was first identified as a type of phobia in a study by Marks and Gelder on the different ages of onset in varieties of phobia (1966). They described social phobia as fear of eating, drinking, blushing, speaking, writing, or vomiting in the presence of other people. Two decades later, Liebowitz and his colleagues (1985) complained that this common disorder was still being neglected. In 1991, Ross cited recent survey data showing that social phobia affects 2.4 million adults in America and that more than 5 million can expect to develop a social phobia during their lifetime. The same survey indicated that fewer than 23 percent of Americans with any type of phobia have received treatment for it. Ross adds: "It is also apparent that there is a lack of public awareness and a lack of clinical knowledge among health care professionals about social phobia" (44). An event that brought social phobia greater public attention was a 1987 appearance on ABC-TV's "Nightline" by Willard Scott, the famed weather reporter on NBC-TV's "Today Show." Scott discussed the anxiety he experienced before and during his television appearances each morning. His comments prompted 20,000 viewers to write letters to the Anxiety Disorders Association of America. Scott was a member of its board of directors at the time.

Ross notes that many of these letter writers "told heartrending stories of their own plight with panic disorder and/or social phobia, describing the frustration of running from one doctor to the next without ever having been given a proper diagnosis or having received help, or missed career and family opportunities, of turning to alcohol, or having suffered bouts of depression, and of suicide ideation and attempts" (44). One person wrote: "I'm thirty-two years old, and I've been living in a hell of almost eighteen years. My social phobia has been the cause of my alcohol abuse. My drinking was the only thing that made me feel comfortable in public; although I don't actually like drinking, I had to." Another had this to say: "I am nineteen years old now. I am a high school dropout because I am extremely shy until I am vulnerable. I seriously need help but I don't have a job, my mother's unemployed, and no one supports me. I want a job. I am going to trade school, but I'll soon give it up because I suffer each day from this illness and I cry to myself a lot. I have thought about ending my life several times." A third related: "I have trouble being around people and certain situations. I have used alcohol to medicate myself. I'm thirty-nine years old and haven't worked around people for years. I have a friend who has a small cleaning service where I can clean houses without anyone being there. I always was very active and outgoing and had tons of friends. I worked in a hospital for four years. People always told me I should have gone to school to be a social worker. They say I have an unusual insight and way with people. They say I have the best common sense of anyone they have ever known. I know that I never reached my potential because of this. I would like to get well and then help others like myself." These are tragic stories, and they are not at all uncommon.

What exactly is social phobia? Greist describes it this way: "The core feature of social phobia is marked and persistent fear of embarrassment or humiliation in social situations where the individual worries that others may judge his or her performance as too much or too little...Onset is usually around puberty; its course is chronic with comorbid depressions common and alcohol and other substances routinely abused in misguided attempts to minimize anxiety and depressive symptoms" (1995, 5). Social phobia may take various forms. The most common "is a fear of public speaking or other public performance such as reading in church, acting in a play, or performing with a musical instrument" (6). Individuals with a fear of public speaking or other public performance "grow anxious that they will not be able to remember or find the words to express their thoughts. This difficulty leads to feelings of embarrassment or humiliation. Others fear they will blush or have noticeable trembling of their hands or head or quavering speech that will disclose their anxiety and lead to embarrassment or humiliation. Still others fear perspiration on their brow or through their clothing will be a visible display of their discomfort. Any or all of these signals might alert their audience and increase their anxiety to the point that their functioning is *actually* impaired" (6).

Another form of social phobia involves eating with others: "While flushing or sweating may signal anxiety, the appearance of tremor most often terrorizes these individuals. As they move food from their plate, bowl, or cup to their mouths, tremor with accompanied spillage might become apparent and lead to embarrassment or humiliation" (6). Others fear writing in public: "They may find it difficult to sign a check at the checkout counter in a supermarket, worrying that a tremulous script may be thought by the clerk to signify funds insufficient to cover the check and cause embarrassment and humiliation" (6). Public restrooms are another social phobia setting for some: "Standing in front of a urinal, males may find their urinary sphincter clamping tightly shut.

Because these social phobic males find it embarrassing to stand too long while others are waiting behind them, they forego urinating" (6). Women who have bathroom anxiety "are more often concerned that their performance will be overheard and will lead to embarrassment. They sometimes use the tactic of turning on a hot air hand dryer or a water faucet to cover the sound of their performance" (6).

Greist concludes that the unifying theme in social phobia is "a fear of performing poorly in a social situation." He also notes that socially phobic individuals share certain characteristics: "Social phobics are, in general, rejection-sensitive. If they are depressed, rejection-sensitivity increases. They are preoccupied with others' views of them and often misinterpret and exaggerate these views. Social phobics have a greater fear of negative evaluation than most people. They are also less assertive than others, at least in their socially phobic situations. Low self-esteem is common, probably because socially phobic individuals have good insight into the inappropriateness and excessiveness of their anxiety and its effects on their lives" (6).

Significantly, social phobics do not lack interest in being with other people. They "long for social contact and comfort in social situations and, by definition, have been able to establish at least one, and often several, age-appropriate social relationships outside their families" (8). Unlike persons with a specific phobia (for example, fear of snakes), they do not—often cannot—avoid stressful and social interactions. Thus, their distress is not about escaping an impending physical assault, as specific phobics usually describe their plight, but about their difficulty in functioning effectively—or optimally—in social contexts (Cook et al. 1988, 739).

The Role of Anxiety in Social Phobia

As noted, social phobia is classified in the *DSM-IV* under the heading of anxiety disorders (1994, 393–444). The fundamental difference between social phobia and agoraphobia as anxiety disorders is that in the case of social phobia, panic attacks always occur in social situations. In the case of agoraphobia, a person may have a panic attack when alone. Thus, an individual who has not previously had a fear of public speaking may have a panic attack while giving a talk and begin to dread giving presentations. If he has panic attacks only in social performance situations, he is likely to be afflicted with social phobia. Individuals with social phobia fear scrutiny and rarely have a panic attack when alone, whereas individuals with agoraphobia are likely to panic when they are alone, especially when they are without a trusted companion (401). Also, while panic attacks may occur in social phobia, they are far more prevalent in agoraphobia. The fact that social phobics are much less likely to panic makes it more difficult to diagnose, however, for a panic attack is self-evident to the person who is afflicted and usually involves or instigates a request for help.

The fact that social phobia is included under the heading of "anxiety disorders" in the *DSM-IV* raises the obvious question: What *is* anxiety? The most common dictionary definition is "a state of being uneasy, or worried about what may happen." Anxiety that reaches clinically significant levels is described as "an unpleasant emotional state experienced as fear or something close to it. It is unconnected with or disproportionate to environmental threats, and is associated with bodily discomforts such as chest constriction, difficulty in breathing, tightness in the throat, and weakness in the legs" (Lewis 1970, 33). The central feature of anxiety is that it is "an emotion directed in anticipation of the future, to ordeals which are yet to come" (33). Occasionally, it is also retroactive in that it may occur after a person emerges from the ordeal (for example, when she begins to shake *after* a public performance). Such apparent exceptions, however, tend to support the general rule that anxiety is an anticipatory emotion. Anxiety is felt in anticipation of real or imagined future events, and it often increases as phobic situations approach. As Roth and Argyle point out, anxiety has an "element of tormenting doubt, that the highly improbable hazards that one dreads may materialize. The anguished anticipation that the impossible may just happen, is at the kernel of morbid states of anxiety" (1988, 35). In a study by Holt and Andrews (1989), however, it was found that social phobics acknowledged having only the *first* of the following "apprehensive expectations": (1) persisting nervousness; (2) fear of death or dying; and (3) fear of a nervous breakdown. In contrast, panic disorder patients subscribed in significant numbers to all three while general anxiety disorder patients subscribed in significant numbers to the first two. Thus, social phobia appears to differ from these other anxiety disorders in that it does not involve catastrophic fears. While we cannot determine from this study whether social phobics' persisting nervousness is more or less severe than that experienced by the other anxiety disorder groups, we *may* conclude that the primary form of anxiety that social phobics experience is a persisting nervousness in anticipation of some future experience or event. Since social phobia concerns social situations, the anticipated events are social ones, and the symptoms that social phobics most often report are restlessness, trouble sleeping, and difficulty concentrating (Reich et al. 1988).

Social phobics also differ from persons with panic disorders in that they usually know what is causing their anxiety. Unlike agoraphobics, persons afflicted with social phobia are generally able to cite experiences that they believe to have triggered their phobia. They typically cite a traumatizing experience in the past that accounts for their apprehension about entering a similar situation in the future. Whether these were in fact the original causes of their disorder is almost impossible to determine. The fact that they believe there is a cause or reason for their phobia, however, distinguishes them from those who are subject to panic attacks, as it enables them to "make sense" of their phobia. That persons subject to panic are unable to make sense of their disorder is not surprising, because panic is a condition that seems to defy all efforts to make sense of it. Unlike social and specific phobias, which arise when certain conditions are met (e.g., an approaching social event or the presence of a snake), a panic attack may occur spontaneously, without warning or evident cause. Thus, researchers believe that the *fear* of having a panic attack is responsible for the agoraphobic's fear of public places, highways, airplanes, and so forth. These places or situations are not the cause of fear. Instead, agoraphobics fear what may happen to them should a panic attack occur in these settings rather than, say, a panic attack at home. In contrast, social phobics' anxiety is due to their anticipation of a particular social situation, which is perceived more as an ordeal to be undergone or avoided than as a situation in which one might have a heart attack or suffer a nervous breakdown. This is not to minimize the potential severity of the anxiety the social phobic may experience, but it indicates that the social phobic's anxiety is situation specific.

To illustrate just how specific this situation might be, a reader's response to an article in a denominational publication for clergy is quite instructive. The author of the original article had argued against the use of personal names in the celebration of holy communion ("Wilma, the body of Christ, given for you") because this practice diverts attention from the corporate nature of the sacrament. This article drew many responses from the magazine's readership, including the following from a pastor who had discontinued the practice of referring to communicants by name: "In my first parish, I found myself dreading communion Sundays because I literally feared that I would forget the name of one or more of the members whom I knew very well. This did happen to me on occasion and my fear was realized." He now defends his discontinuance of the practice on the grounds that it brings attention to the pastor instead of the Christ who gave his life for the communicants:

"Do we use the person's name as a way of making the sacrament more personal, or do we use their name as a way of bringing attention to ourselves? Comments like, 'Pastor, how do you remember so many names? I'm sure I couldn't do that!' come to mind. It's nice to get 'feel-good strokes' for our ego, but my point is just that: If we would be honest with ourselves, we use their names because it brings attention to us."

It may be an exaggeration to say that this clergyman was afflicted with a social phobia, but his description of his anticipation of communion Sundays strongly suggests this. The ordeal of having to remember the names of everyone and his fear that he would forget one or two certainly made him anxious. He uses the word "dread" to describe his emotional state, and in order to emphasize the severity of his anxiety, he says that he "literally feared" he would forget someone's name. Apparently his anxiety was strong enough that it actually impaired his ability to remember names on some occasions. His theological rationale for discontinuing the practice is noteworthy, as he reframes the fear of embarrassing oneself by means of a theological statement about the dangers of egotism, of wanting to be the center of attention. While this theological rationale was mentioned by several others who responded to the original article, it has special poignance in his case, since the "attention" he received on those Sundays that he forgot one or two names was anything but an ego-builder. I would guess that on these occasions he experienced much embarrassment and felt himself to be negatively judged by members of his congregation. He now has a theological rationale for the avoidance of this specific social situation that earlier caused so much anxiety. What should interest us here, however, is not the question of whether his theological rationale is a convenient defense for his having discontinued the feared practice, but the fact that his anxiety was so specific. It was not the act of celebrating holy communion itself that caused anxiety but the idea that he would need to be able to remember everyone's name as he celebrated holy communion. This should alert us to the fact that the anxiety felt by social phobics may result from very specific features of a dreaded future event. In turn, this may explain why one may have a phobic reaction to one public speaking situation and not another, or one informal social gathering and not another, even though both situations or gatherings may appear to someone else to be identical.

Fear Response in Social Phobia

So far, we have considered social phobia as a type of anxiety disorder and have noted that the key feature of social phobia is the anticipation of a dreaded social situation. Unlike persons who are merely nervous or somewhat apprehensive, the social phobic *dreads* the approaching situation and seriously considers and often devises ways to avoid it altogether. We may wonder, however, why the word "phobia" is attached to this particular form of anxiety. Phobia implies fear. The most common dictionary definition of phobia is that it is "an irrational, excessive, and persistent *fear* of some particular thing or situation."

But what precisely is fear, and what does it mean to say that a person "fears" a social situation? In his article on anxiety and phobia, Williams (1987) raises some important questions about the use of the word "fear" to describe the behaviors that occur in social phobia. He points out that we normally view fear as a subjective feeling, which raises a problem in the case of social phobia because subjective feelings of fear are highly variable among phobics: "Some terminate attempts to perform a phobic activity although they are not feeling particularly afraid, whereas others perform a large number of approach tasks long after they have become extremely fearful" (165). Avoidance behavior without fear is commonplace: "If people know that a well-practiced and easily executed avoidance response will remove a particular problem, they have little reason to fear," and, therefore, "subjective fear clearly is not the major determinant of dysfunctional behavior" (165–166). Williams doubts that the word "fear" should be used in reference to social phobia.

However, a persuasive case for its use has been formulated by Arne Öhman (1986), a clinical psychologist at the University of Uppsala. Öhman applies what he calls a "functional-evolutionary perspective" to fear. He points out that humans' encounters with large and/or threatening animals have been a recurrent fear throughout the history of humanity. A second type of encounter, also recurrent throughout human history and also reflecting fear, is "the one between humans facing each other in anger and distress" (124). He suggests that encounters with threatening animals and angry humans have important structural similarities: "In both cases it is appropriate to speak about an attacker and a defendant. The encounters are competitive, and although few combatants in actual reality get themselves killed, the outcome is potentially deadly. The stakes involved make it appropriate to speak about both kinds of situations as emotional or stressful" (124).

But what kinds of emotions are involved here? Öhman says that most of us would agree that the *human* attacker may be described in terms of anger and aggression. We are less certain that an animal confronting a human is acting out of anger or aggression, because it is equally possible that the animal is attacking out of fear. On the other hand, we do not hesitate to apply the label of *fear* to any defendants, animal or human, who *yield* to the superior power of the attacker and make their escape. Thus, fear is associated with avoidance behavior, but attack behavior is more ambiguous, since an animal may attack a human because the animal is afraid. Focusing on avoidance behavior, which is far more typical of social phobia than attack behavior, Öhman questions whether human individuals who escape from hostilities with other humans are really experiencing the same emotion as humans making their escape from attacking animals. On closer inspection, the defendants in these two types of battles, in spite of approximately equal levels of fear in the two situations, would have different reactions. The person escaping from the animal is likely to feel very much relieved and as a rebound effect of the fear state is likely to experience relaxation or even exuberant joy. Escaping from a vicious dog is a case in point. When one yields to a human aggressor, however, "there is a fair likelihood that the associated feelings would be of humiliation and defeat," and perhaps one would agonize over having "lost face" (124). In fact, while few humans would ever hesitate to escape from a threatening animal, many males prefer to get themselves killed than to reveal their fear by fleeing from a human opponent. Öhman cites a study of homicides in Detroit where about half the men killed in social conflicts were victims in altercations of trivial origin, where little but "face" was at stake. He concludes that the ostensibly similar fear states experienced in encounters with animal predators and hostile humans show important differences (124).

How does this relate to phobias? If we extend the distinction between the fear state experienced in encounters with animal predators and hostile humans to intense, irrational, and nonadaptive fears, we have a basis for identifying important differences between animal phobias and social phobia. We may also account for their characteristic age of onset. Animal phobias (which fall under the general heading of "specific phobias") are generally believed to be the first of the three major phobia groups to develop. Age of onset is usually in early or middle childhood. Thus, Öhman notes that while infants typically are kept close to protecting parents, children who are mature enough to make exploratory escapades of their own but lack the effective antipredatory strategies of the fully mature animal are especially at risk. Therefore, "from a biological point of view, one would expect the childhood years to be a period of especially easy acquisition of animal fears" (129).

In contrast, social phobia usually has an onset in the mid-teens, typically emerging out of a childhood history of social inhibition or shyness. This means that "while animal fears belong within a somewhat circumscribed behavior system, social fears occur as a component of a larger behavioral system." Thus, one may escape a threatening social situation but believe one has been cowardly or otherwise weak for doing so. Also, because social fear develops between humans, "social fear is only one pole of a system that includes social dominance at the other end" (129). In Öhman's view, the function of the dominance/submissiveness system is to establish social order. When relatively stable hierarchies have been established within a group, there is a marked decrease in antagonistic encounters, which is favorable for group cohesiveness and the group's functioning as a social unit. Establishing dominance hierarchies is therefore a way of reconciling the conflicts between individual and social motives within the group (129–130).

Öhman suggests that social phobics are highly sensitive to the dominance/submissiveness system in the social order, and that they have considerable fear of its ability to victimize them. They enter social situations with the anticipation that they will occasion dominating behaviors directed at themselves, to which they will instinctively submit. Why submit? Because they are behaviorally incapable of responding to dominating behavior by counterdominating behaviors designed to place their opponents in the submissive position. Social phobics expect from such social situations that they will inevitably "lose face," and this is what their fear is essentially about. What makes their fear more or less irrational is that they enter social situations with anxious anticipation. That is, they have a predisposition or preparedness to be threatened by the dominance/submissiveness system that is integral to most social situations but is unlikely to make this particular individual its target on each and every occasion. The anticipation or preparedness for an experience of losing face is what makes the social phobic's fear seem irrational. The social phobic is especially likely to believe that he—not someone else—will be the victim of the dominant member of the group, that he will be the person they will pick on, make fun of, or otherwise cause to look ridiculous, ill-prepared, or out of place.

Öhman's theory fits well with certain characteristics of social phobia, including the social phobic's tendency to be highly self-conscious, as though she is being carefully observed and sized up by others, and the tendency to be nonassertive. His theory also helps to explain why social phobics experience little or no anxiety in their family relationships or with a group of very close friends, since these social situations are ones in which the dominance/submissiveness system may be only minimally present or, if present may actually operate in favor of the social phobic (that is, *he*, as the parent, may be dominant in these situations).

Öhman's analysis of the role that dominance hierarchies play in social situations indicates that social phobics' fear is that of losing social face, of experiencing embarrassment or humiliation. This fear may have its origins in a "history of defeats," of earlier social situations in which one was placed on the defensive by dominating persons. As a result, the social phobic has learned to assume the submissive position even without provocation. To take this submissive position even before being challenged to do so becomes her strategy for survival. Expectations by other group members that the social phobic may actually assume the dominant position in a given social situation because of his senior status, greater competence, and so forth, are frustrated, since the social phobic has little desire to assume the dominant social role, having become adept at the submissive role. Such lack of desire to assume this role may, however, cause others to believe he is lazy, lacks ambition, or does not in fact possess the competence ascribed to him, while he may feel frustrated, even angry, that others who are less competent and knowledgeable exert greater influence over the group. His helplessness to do anything about the situation is perhaps the most frustrating thing of all.

The social phobic's dilemma is the fact that avoiding social situations in which one may lose face is virtually impossible. However, an even more distressing dilemma is that social phobics know that their fears are to a considerable extent unfounded or irrational. Therefore, each and every decision to attend or avoid a social function that evokes anticipatory anxiety confronts them with the basic irrationality of their fears. If they decide to avoid a particular social situation because of this anticipatory anxiety, they must then live with the secret knowledge that there was no good, rational reason why it was avoided. This suggests that there is a "secret shame" that underlies the more overt fear of embarrassment and humiliation experienced by social phobics. This experience of secret shame becomes a vicious cycle, because it contributes to the low self-confidence that Öhman associates with the social submissive system.

Thus, Öhman's emphasis on the dominance/submissiveness system in the social order enables us to see that if fear is defined as a reaction to physical threat, then the word "fear" is inappropriate, since the dominance/submissiveness system is actually designed to eliminate physical threat. It is the feature of a human social system that keeps us from physically threatening one another. If fear means fear of "losing face," of suffering embarrassment or humiliation, however, then fear is certainly involved in social phobia. What makes social phobia more threatening than fear of animals, where perceived physical threat *is* involved, is that for social phobia, avoidance is not as effective a coping strategy as for animal fears. One may succeed in isolating oneself from a feared animal and live a normal human existence. This is not the case with social phobia, where isolation from all human interaction is not only impossible but highly dysfunctional. Thus, social phobics often force themselves to participate in feared situations precisely because they have a greater fear of the consequences of isolation from all human interaction. Few humans are able to live like hermits. More importantly, social phobics do not want to live an isolated existence. They value human interaction.

Öhman gives particular attention to social phobia and one form of specific phobias, using animal phobia to shed light on the fear involved in social phobia. He also comments on agoraphobia, however, conceding that agoraphobia does not fit his basic model centered on the dominance/submissiveness system. This, he believes, is no accident, "since at least at the theoretical level one could advance a convincing argument that agoraphobia has a unique evolutionary origin, related to separation anxiety, which sets it apart from other phobias" (127–128). The theory that separation anxiety (e.g., the child's fear of being left by his mother in his preschool classroom) is central to agoraphobia has been a popular one because it appears to be consistent with the fact that agoraphobics are markedly more fearful when they are completely alone than when they are in the company of another. Many agoraphobics totally avoid being alone, and others require the presence of a companion, especially when attempting to venture beyond their "safety zones." Usually, this companion is a particular family member, most commonly one's spouse, but a nonhuman attachment object such as a pet may also be of assistance. As Routh and Bernholtz (1991) point out, the similarity of this fear of being alone to separation anxiety, where the young child may use an attachment object (such as a teddy bear or prized blanket) as a secure base for exploration, is certainly striking. They also note that efforts to help agoraphobics do not focus on challenging the patient to *approach* crowds or open places. Instead, they involve the more cautious approach of encouraging the patient to walk away from "safety," to take a step or two out from safe places or safe persons (303). This appears to be reminiscent of small children's first experiences of walking away from the safety provided by their mothers or other caregivers.

On the other hand, the separation anxiety theory has been challenged because empirical efforts to establish that agoraphobia, whose onset is usually in the mid- to late twenties, may be traced to separation anxiety in early childhood have had mixed results. For example, the argument that agoraphobics are more likely to have experienced school phobia (refused to go to school) in childhood has not been supported. Nor have agoraphobics been found to have experienced greater rates of parental death in childhood than nonagoraphobics (Thyer et al. 1988). Also, while phobics in general assert that one or both parents were emotionally cold or rejecting, there is no evidence to indicate that the parents of agoraphobics differed significantly in this regard from parents of other types of phobics.

Still, Öhman's is an evolution-based theory, which means that fear of leaving a safe place and entering a place not known to be safe may be as much a part of our prehistory as the fear of animal predators and hostile humans. Thus, despite the fact that evidence that agoraphobics experienced greater separation anxiety in early childhood is inconclusive, the idea that agoraphobia involves separation anxiety is valuable because it helps to identify the nature of the fear that is unique to agoraphobia. The agoraphobic experiences something like what small children experience when they venture outside the holding environment created for them by their parent (Kohut 1984). The agoraphobic's experience of panic, the fear of losing all self-control, of self-disintegration, of the possibility that one could suffer death itself, are all prefigured in the separation anxiety of the small child. What these characteristics of agoraphobia mean for social phobia is that sensitivity to the dominance/ submissiveness system in social groups distinguishes social phobia from the other major types of phobia. The social phobic especially experiences anxiety when required to assume the dominant position, or when those who are dominant behave in a manner—autocratic, abusive— that provokes the desire among submissive members of the group to protest, causing the social phobic to want to speak out while experiencing an inability to do so.

Shyness and Susceptibility to Social Phobia

One of the most important questions that researchers have recently raised is whether individuals have a temperamental predisposition to develop social phobia. Most social phobics identify a specific traumatic experience or event that, in their view, marks the onset of their phobia. The social phobic selects from his "history of defeats" an experience that is most memorable, probably because it was especially painful, in that the emotion of shame was particularly potent (Kaufman and Raphael 1996, 60–63). While there is little reason to doubt that these experiences have contributed to the development of the phobia, we may also wonder whether the socially phobic person had a predisposition toward social phobia and was therefore more negatively affected by these experiences than someone without this predisposition would have been.

Research on social phobia indicates that there are several predisposing factors in the development of the phobia. Family history is one such predisposing factor. Gender also seems to be a factor. The content and prevalence of phobias also vary with culture and ethnicity. Race may also be a factor. I will discuss these in more detail in the next chapter. However, the fact that social phobics anticipate that they will assume the submissive role in the dominance/submissiveness social system suggests that there is a more deeply rooted temperamental predisposition to become socially phobic. Rosenbaum et al. (1991) argue that anxiety disorders are like other medical disorders for which an individual may have a predisposition. They focus on the developmental aspects of panic disorder and social phobia, in particular the possibility that "behavioral inhibition" in children may be a precursor to phobic disorders in adults. Their investigation of longitudinal studies at the Harvard Infant Study Laboratory indicate that 10 to 15 percent of Caucasian American children are predisposed to be irritable as infants, shy and fearful as toddlers, and cautious, quiet, and introverted when they reach school age. Over several years, Kagan and his coworkers at the Harvard laboratory have studied two independent groups of children selected at twenty-one and thirty-one months of age. One group was judged to be "behaviorally inhibited," the other "behaviorally uninhibited" when exposed to unfamiliar settings, people, and objects. Follow-up studies at four, five, and seven and a half years of age revealed that these differences in behavior did not significantly change. For example, a child's tendency to approach or withdraw from novelty reflects an enduring temperamental trait.

Kagan and his colleagues (1987) had postulated that physiological factors would be involved and would account in part for the differences between inhibited and uninhibited children's behaviors. The behavioral responses of retreat and avoidance, along with lowered voice, marked behavioral restraint, and increased heart rate, all found among the inhibited children, supported this hypothesis. Rosenbaum and his coauthors conclude that these observations by Kagan and his colleagues. "suggested that behavioral inhibition in infancy might be one marker of anxiety proneness" (6). Thus, they hypothesized that behavioral inhibition in infancy "could represent one possibly inherited physiologic predisposition to the development of anxiety psychopathology." A temperamental predisposition to "experience distress and increased tendency to appraise new situations as more threatening" could therefore "set the stage for the onset of anxiety disorders later in life" (6).

To test this hypothesis, they sent fifty-six children, aged two to seven years, to the Harvard laboratory to be tested, observed, and rated with respect to their behavioral inhibition. These children, together with the children who had originally been studied by Kagan and his coworkers, were compared with children making routine pediatric outpatient clinic visits to the Massachusetts General Hospital. Using structured diagnostic interviews, Rosenbaum and his colleagues found that inhibited children "had increased risks for multiple anxiety disorders, overanxious disorders, and phobic disorders." The children who had been identified as inhibited at twenty-one months in the original studies by Kagan and colleagues were eight years old at the time that they were retested. Phobic symptoms reported by these children included fears of standing up and speaking in front of class, strangers, crowds, being called on in class, elevators, plane travel, going outside alone, and being upstairs and home alone, all symptoms reminiscent of adult agoraphobia and social phobia (7).

Rosenbaum and colleagues caution that only longitudinal studies can definitively indicate whether these early response patterns are specifically linked to risk for developing anxiety disorders across the life span. But they conclude that anxiety proneness, "manifested early in life, interacts with developmental experiences and life events to determine risk on onset of anxiety disorder" (9).

While Kagan and his coworkers refer to the children in their studies as "behaviorally inhibited," they also use the more traditional word, "shyness" (Kagan & Reznick 1986). Similarly, in their discussion of social phobia, Beidel and Morris (1995) suggest that *sociability* and *shyness* are two contrasting traits that are detectable at a very early age and are stable across periods of developmental change. They define sociability as "a preference for affiliation and the companionship of others rather than solitude," while shyness is "a form of social withdrawal characterized by social-evaluative concerns, particularly in novel settings."(That is, shyness is manifest with strangers but not with family members.) Thus, "sociability refers to the desire for social affiliation, whereas shyness refers to distress and inhibited behaviors in social interactions" (181). They note that some persons are low on the sociability dimension, having little desire for and receiving very little satisfaction from social interaction with others. In social encounters they may not interact but, on the other hand, they show or feel very little emotional distress. Others may have a strong desire for social encounters but become so distressed when in the company of other people that they are unable to engage in rewarding interpersonal interactions. Children who profess a desire for social encounters but who become significantly distressed when doing so may meet diagnostic criteria for social phobia (181). Thus, shyness found in children who *are* sociable places them at risk for social phobia. In effect, social phobia, temperamentally speaking, is based on a paradox. Children at risk for future social phobia are both sociable *and* shy.

In another study of developmental factors in childhood and adolescent shyness, Bruch and Cheek (1995) note that shyness is the normal personality characteristic that most closely parallels social phobia, in that both share the antecedent fear of negative evaluation. On the other hand, while shyness and social phobia share cognitive and affective manifestations of fear of negative evaluation, this does not mean that they are synonymous, since social phobia may involve a more pervasive pattern than shyness of avoidance and impairment in social functioning. Still, research on the origins of childhood shyness has identified a number of reliable factors predictive of stable patterns of shyness over substantial time periods (163). These authors cite a study by Kagan and Reznick (1986) showing that certain children appear to be born with a biological predisposition to shyness. They also agree with Buss (1980, 1986), however, who distinguishes between an early-developing fearful shyness and a later-developing self-conscious shyness. The fearful type typically emerges during the first year of life and is reflected by temperamental qualities of wariness, emotionality, and behavioral inhibition, whereas the self-conscious type appears around ages four to five and peaks between ages fourteen to seventeen as adolescents cope with identity issues (166). In addition to the physical anxiety and behavioral inhibition that characterize early-developing shyness, later-developing shyness also involves such symptoms of psychic anxiety as painful self-consciousness and negative self-preoccupation.

Surveys employing retrospective reports of college students support this developmental conceptualization of shyness. In studies conducted by Bruch and Cheek (1995) and their colleagues, it has been found that about 75 percent of those who were shy in early childhood remain shy, while only 50 percent of those who were first shy during late childhood or adolescence are currently shy. Thus, there is a greater likelihood that early shyness will persist into adulthood, a fact that directly counters the popular view of shyness as something that young children will eventually outgrow. Early-developing shyness also appears to be more of an adjustment problem, with males reporting the most behavioral symptoms of shyness.

Finally, Bruch and Cheek note that shy children and adolescents are more likely to experience negative peer relationships. A major reason for this is that "the shy child's inhibition and withdrawal is perceived as deviant from age-appropriate social behavior by the peer group and is reacted to by responses of neglect, rejection, or victimization (e.g., bullying)" (174). This difficulty in peer relationships is congruent with Öhman's view that social phobics are especially sensitive to the dominance/submissiveness system in the social order, for peer relationships are ones where the "dominant" and "submissive" roles are extremely fluid, which is much less the case in parent-child and teacher-child relationships. The shy child is likely to play the submissive role to a disproportionate degree while the uninhibited child will disproportionately play the dominant one. Shy children are therefore most likely to be threatened by social situations where the social hierarchy is not well-established, where members vie for power and influence. Shy children rely on the protective structures of preestablished dominance/submissiveness systems (parent-child, teacher-child) as these are often used to bring sanctions against the uninhibited child who dominates or bullies the shy, inhibited child. On the other hand, shy children find it threatening to be thrust into the position of dominance, as occurs, for example, when they are asked to speak or perform before an audience of their peers. A teacher's effort to "help" the shy child assume a position of dominance may therefore fail to have the intended effect. In fact, it may solidify the shy child's submissiveness because such encouragement to assume the dominant role elicits an overpowering anxiety.

Conclusion

This chapter has focused on the fact that social phobia is classified as an anxiety disorder and is considered one of the three major types of phobias. My primary concern has been to locate social phobia within the larger framework of anxiety disorders and the more circumscribed schema of phobia types. I have also been concerned with some of the more tantalizing and vexing theoretical issues that social phobia raises, including the question of how social phobia develops, why it persists over time, and why it is so resistant to extinction or remission.

In the course of this discussion, I have noted that shame has a great deal to do with social phobia both because social phobics are concerned that they will experience embarrassment or humiliation and because they understand that their avoidance of certain social situations is without rational foundation. I have also explored the role of fear in social phobia and have emphasized that the fear involved is that of losing face. This fear of losing face indicates that the central feature of social situations for social phobics is their dominance/submissiveness system. That social phobics are especially sensitive to the dominance/submissiveness system accounts for many of the characteristics of social phobia that are otherwise difficult to reconcile with one another (such as the fact that social phobics are comfortable in some social situations but not in others). Finally, I have treated favorably the developmental literature on shyness, as I think it goes far toward accounting for the temperamental predisposition toward adult social phobia. Unfortunately, it also makes it harder to believe that social phobia is easily curable.

CHAPTER 2

The Diagnosis of Social Phobia

In this chapter I will be concerned with issues in the diagnosis of social phobia. Particular attention will be given to the criteria for determining whether an individual is socially phobic and to the predisposing factors that place an individual at risk for social phobia. A key resource in the diagnosis of social phobia is the *DSM-IV*, which reflects the research findings of the past decade and represents the collective wisdom of researchers and clinicians pertaining to the diagnosis of social phobia. While the *DSM-IV* is designed to assist clinicians in determining whether a given client or patient is a social phobic, it is also useful for identifying individuals who may not qualify for the diagnosis of social phobia but who have similar phobic tendencies.

Two Diagnostic Issues: Criteria and Severity

The Diagnostic Criteria for Social Phobia

The *DSM-IV* identifies the diagnostic criteria that clinicians use to determine whether a given individual suffers from social phobia. The first criterion, viewed as an essential feature of social phobia, is "a marked and persistent fear of one or more social or performance situations in which the person is exposed to unfamiliar people or to scrutiny by others. The individual fears that he or she will act in a way (or show anxiety symptoms) that will be humiliating or embarrassing" (1994, 416). The second criterion is that "exposure to the social or performance situation almost invariably provokes an immediate anxiety response" (417). This response may take the form of a panic attack, but if it does, the panic attack is directly related to the specific situation that provokes the anxiety. This is in contrast to agoraphobia, where panic attacks may occur more randomly and not necessarily in relation to certain feared situations. The third criterion is that the individual recognizes that the "fear is excessive or unreasonable" (417). The fourth criterion is that "most often, the social or performance situation is avoided, although it is sometimes endured with dread" (417). These are the four main diagnostic criteria for social phobia. They are found in virtually all cases of social phobias among adults. They may be viewed as experiential stages in the phobic process, as the person initially fears exposure, which provokes anticipatory anxiety, which elicits the realization that the fear is greater than the situation demands, a recognition that has little influence on (i.e., doesn't alter or change) the determination to avoid the situation or endure it with dread. The fact that criterion four (avoidance or endurance with dread) occurs in spite of criterion three (knowing that the fear is excessive or unreasonable) accounts for the judgment that the process is a phobic one.

Besides these four basic criteria, there are several others that are also important because they enable the clinician to take the special circumstances of the individual into account. Thus, the fifth criterion is that the diagnosis is appropriate "only if the avoidance, fear, or anxious anticipation of encountering the social or performance situation interferes with the person's daily routine, occupational functioning, or social life, or if the person is markedly distressed about having the phobia" (417). Thus, if a person has a marked fear of speaking or performing before an audience, but her job or profession never requires her to act in these ways, she would not qualify as a social phobic under the *DSM-IV* diagnostic guidelines. Functional impairment is therefore an important diagnostic consideration. If this criterion, however, is applied too rigidly (that is, if only those who must speak before a group as a condition of their job or profession were considered socially phobic), the numbers of persons who are afflicted with social phobia and/ or the severity of their affliction may be seriously underestimated. For example, attendance at informal social gatherings may not be a requisite for a particular job, but the person who *is* able to engage in these informal gatherings may receive more positive evaluations from a boss or employer than the person who avoids such gatherings. Also, knowing that she has a fear of social gatherings or speaking in public may cause a person to decide in advance not to pursue a given profession even though she has the necessary qualifications for it. Henry James, the novelist, dropped out of law school because he felt (and others confirmed) that he had performed badly in mock court. Throughout his life, he feared speaking to a formal audience, though he was considered a fine conversationalist at small dinner parties. (His social phobia may also have contributed to his observational skills, a prominent feature of his novels.)

The sixth criterion applies to individuals under eighteen years of age and states that the duration of the fear must be at least six months. This criterion is especially useful in the case of children or adolescents who are going through a difficult adjustment period, such as moving to a new school or experiencing a family crisis. Children and adolescents may develop socially phobic symptoms during these periods, but a diagnosis of social phobia is not warranted unless they continue for six months or more.

The seventh criterion is that the fear or avoidance is not due to the direct physiological effects of a substance (a drug of abuse or medication) or a general medical condition. Many social phobics do in fact make use of substances, especially alcohol, to help them get through anxiety-provoking social situations. This diagnostic criterion, however, cautions that social phobic symptoms may be the *result* of the physiological effects of substances and medicines, and therefore a diagnosis of social phobia is not warranted.

The eighth criterion is that if a general medical condition or another mental disorder *is* present, the social fear needs to be unrelated to this condition. Thus, if an individual trembles as a result of Parkinson's disease or exhibits abnormal eating behavior such as anorexia nervosa or bulimea nervosa and fears certain social situations for this reason, diagnosis of social phobia is inappropriate because the social anxiety or avoidance is better accounted for by the medical condition itself.

The foregoing criteria apply to adults and adolescents. They are also applicable to children, but in this case various qualifiers need to be taken into account. For example, concerning the first criterion of marked and persistent fear, the mere fact that a child fears exposure to unfamiliar people or possible scrutiny by others is insufficient basis for a diagnosis of social phobia. There must also be evidence of the capacity for "age-appropriate social relationships with familiar people," and "the anxiety must occur in peer settings, not just in interactions with adults" (414). Concerning the second criterion that there must be an immediate anxiety response, the anxiety may be expressed by children through "crying, tantrums, freezing, or shrinking from social situations with unfamiliar people" (417). With regard to the third criterion, children need not be able to recognize that their fear is excessive or unreasonable.

The *DSM-IV* provides descriptions and illustrations of the distress that social phobics experience. For example, it notes that individuals with social phobia experience "concerns about embarrassment" and "are afraid that others will judge them to be anxious, weak, 'crazy,' or 'stupid'" (412). Social phobics may fear public speaking because of concern that "others will notice their trembling hands or voice" or they may experience extreme anxiety "when conversing with others because of the fear that they will appear inarticulate" (412). They may avoid eating, drinking, or writing in public because of a fear "of being embarrassed by having others see their hands shake" (412). Persons with social phobia almost always experience symptoms of anxiety, such as palpitations, tremors, sweating, gastrointestinal discomfort, diarrhea, muscle tension, blushing, and confusion. In severe cases, these symptoms may meet the criteria for a panic attack.

Adults and adolescents with social phobia recognize that their fear of one or more social situations is excessive or unreasonable. Thus, social phobics are differentiated from persons who suffer from delusional disorder (for example, a person who will not eat in public because he is convinced that he will be observed by the local police). The *DSM-IV* recognizes that there are social situations in which an individual's fear is not unreasonable, and this may apply even to situations in which no one else feels threatened. For example, a student may fear being called on in class because she is unprepared, or an employee may fear a meeting with his boss because he suspects that its purpose is to announce that he is being fired. Under the circumstances, such fear is not unreasonable, and a diagnosis of social phobia is unwarranted. Conversely, if a student is very well prepared but is mortally afraid that she will be called on by the teacher, or if an employee fears a meeting with the boss during which he expects to receive high commendation, this is basis for a diagnosis of social phobia.

The *DSM-IV* also emphasizes that the fear or avoidance must interfere significantly "with the person's normal routine, occupational or academic functioning, or social activities or relationships," or the person must experience "marked distress about having the phobia" (412). Fears of being embarrassed in social situations are common, but "usually the degree of distress or impairment is insufficient to warrant a diagnosis of social phobia" (412). For most persons with social phobia, the feared situation is quite specific. They either fear speaking or performing before an audience, *or* eating at a social gathering, *or* carrying on a one-to-one conversation with a member of the other sex, and so forth. But the *DSM-IV* has a "generalized social phobia" subcategory for use when a person's fears are related to a variety of social situations (e.g., initiating or maintaining conversations, participating in small groups, dating, speaking to authority figures, attending parties, etc.). Persons with generalized social phobia usually fear public performance situations *and* social interaction situations. They may be more likely than other social phobics to manifest deficits in social skills and to have severe social and work impairment. For those whose social phobia is not so "generalized," feared situations may range from one specific social situation to several but not most social situations (412–413).

The *DSM-IV* emphasizes that embarrassment is involved in social phobia, but merely because a person experiences embarrassment in a given social context is insufficient basis for a diagnosis of social phobia. For example, a person may be deeply embarrassed that he fainted when giving blood or that she was unable to answer a question from the audience in response to her talk or lecture, but these are not grounds for a social phobia diagnosis because a spontaneous moment of embarrassment is not a sign of social phobia. Instead, there must be significant anticipatory anxiety leading a person seriously to consider avoiding the situation. On the other hand, an unanticipated socially embarrassing situation may mark the onset of a social phobia, especially if the individual is already at risk (innately shy).

The *DSM-IV* cautions against an indiscriminant use of the diagnosis of social phobia. It notes that "performance anxiety, stage fright, and shyness in social situations that involve unfamiliar people are common and should not be diagnosed as social phobia unless the anxiety or avoidance leads to clinically significant impairment or marked distress" (416). One clue to whether the anxiety is sufficient to warrant the diagnosis of social phobia is how far in advance of the actual situation the anxiety begins to present itself. In social phobia, marked anticipatory anxiety frequently occurs "far in advance of upcoming social or public situations (e.g., worrying every day for several weeks before attending a social event)" (412). Another is the actual negative effect of the anxiety on a person's performance. In social phobia, "there may be a vicious cycle of anticipatory anxiety leading to fearful cognition and anxiety symptoms in the feared situation, which leads to actual or perceived poor performance in the feared situations, which leads to embarrassment and increased anticipatory anxiety about the feared situation, and so on" (412). Social phobics typically view their situation as a vicious cycle, or as a dilemma—a sort of labyrinth—from which there appears to be no apparent escape.

Finally, the *DSM-IV* addresses the issue of the expected duration of social phobia over the course of a lifetime. It notes that social phobia typically has an onset in the mid-teens, sometimes emerging out of a childhood history of social inhibition or shyness. Some individuals, however, report the onset in early childhood. Onset may abruptly follow a stressful or humiliating experience, or it may develop gradually. In either case, the "course of social phobia is often continuous. Duration is frequently lifelong, although the disorder may attenuate in severity or remit during adulthood" (414). Also, severity of impairment may fluctuate with life stress and demands. For example, social phobia may diminish after a person who fears dating becomes married. It may then reemerge after her spouse's death. Or a job promotion to a position requiring public speaking may result in the emergence of social phobia in someone who previously never needed to speak in public. Thus its "insidious" nature derives from the fact that a person may not know that he has a predisposition to social phobia until changing life circumstances (even positive ones) reveal it; or a person may believe that she has overcome her social phobia only to experience its reemergence when life circumstances change again. As we would expect of a phobia that involves the social dimension of human life, social phobia is therefore very responsive to changing social conditions. At the same time, it has a basis in deeply rooted temperamental factors (especially childhood shyness), which means that it will not necessarily go into remission merely because one's life circumstances have been successfully altered so as to preclude the recurrence of the feared situation.

Severity of Impairment

In their essay on diagnostic issues, Heckelman and Schneier (1995) note that community studies have consistently found that most persons with social phobia do not seek treatment. Moreover, "an even larger pool of persons with extreme fear of embarrassment do not meet criteria for the disorder because their feared situations can be avoided without functional impairment" (8). In their view, this raises questions about the appropriate threshold for determining what constitutes social phobia in any given case. In one study, persons who had reported social anxiety in at least one situation were asked if their discomfort or nervousness in their most anxiety-evoking situation had any negative effect on their life at home, work, or school or had bothered them personally (i.e., caused "marked distress"). Of those who reported social anxiety, 31 percent reported "moderate" or "a great deal" of psychosocial disruption or personal distress; and of these, 12 percent met the more stringent threshold criterion of "a great deal" of disruption or distress. In another study, at least one severely stressful situation was reported by 69 percent of persons interviewed, 40 percent reported two or more situations, and 18 percent reported at least three situations. The authors note that the "large proportion of persons fearing only one situation differs from findings in clinical samples, where most patients fear more than one situation…Fear of multiple situations probably contributes to impairment and to the likelihood of seeking treatment" (9–10).

While the number of types of social situations that a person avoids is one factor in determining the severity of the problem, it does not necessarily address the *degree* of impairment. In some occupations, even if only one type of social situation is avoided, this type may be so central to effective performance of the occupation that it may be severely disabling. The renowned concert pianist Vladimir Horowitz avoided public performances for a whole decade because he feared negative evaluations by the audience. During this period, he continued to make private recordings, indicating that he felt his performance was negatively affected by the presence of an audience. Clergypersons who dread public speaking may find that this is seriously disabling because preaching is a central feature of ministry, especially in the congregational context.

In a study concerned with the degree of functional impairment among social phobics, Turner et al. (1986) concluded that social phobics suffer considerable impairment in their academic, occupational, and social functioning. They found that 83 percent felt that their fear inhibited academic functioning by preventing them from speaking in class, joining clubs or athletic teams, being elected to leadership positions in clubs or student organizations, or by preventing them from getting better grades because of nonparticipation in class discussion; 92 percent felt that their occupational performance was significantly impaired, citing the inability to make informal suggestions in staff meetings and presentations before small or large groups, all resulting in lack of career advancement or being passed over for promotion. In evaluating their general social functioning, 69 percent reported impairment, stating that their fear prohibited them from attending social events connected to their work, joining civic organizations, or being elected to leadership positions in these same organizations. Also, 50 percent of the unmarried persons in the study believed that their social functioning was limited, either by their hesitancy to engage in social activities or by the inability to establish a level of intimacy conducive to long-term relationships. "Thus, social phobia appears to be a disorder resulting in significant impact on life functioning in a majority of those seen in our clinic, and although there was no report of complete incapacitation, significant impairment was highly prevalent" (391).

A more recent study by Davidson et al. (1994) notes that community and clinical studies have established that social phobics carry a heavy burden in that the disorder begins early in life and has a low spontaneous recovery rate. They cite a recent survey that reported that 10.5 percent of the adults reported at least one of the three listed social phobic situations but only 3.8 percent of these fulfilled the diagnostic threshold criteria for social phobia. They compared the subthreshold social phobics with healthy control subjects as well as with diagnosed social phobics and concluded that the subthreshold social phobics were more likely than the control subjects to report work attendance problems, poor grades in school, symptoms of conduct disturbance, impaired subjective social support, lack of self-confidence, lack of a close friend, and greater number of life changes. They conclude that these adults were impaired or disadvantaged in many ways. They also conclude that because most initially rejected the idea that their lives were impaired, they were insufficiently aware of the effects of their fear, either because they had made a lifelong adaptation to a phobic lifestyle, because of the social stigma involved, or for some other reason (982). Thus, even if these individuals do not meet the stricter criteria for social phobia, they are at risk of some kind of functional impairment in their personal and professional lives. The authors encourage clinicians to give attention to these persons and not limit treatment to patients with obvious impairment, and they suggest that researchers should be as willing to study cases below the diagnostic threshold as cases that do meet the standard diagnostic criteria.

Another way to determine the degree of the severity of the problem is to consider what other disorders the individual may have, since other disorders commonly occur with social phobia. Schneier et al. (1992) found that 69 percent of the social phobics in their study had other lifetime mental or emotional problems and that the onset of social phobia occurred first in 77 percent of these cases. The disorders with the highest lifetime prevalence were specific phobia (59 percent), agoraphobia (45 percent), alcohol abuse (19 percent), major depression (17 percent) and drug abuse (13 percent). The association of social phobia with depression has been of particular interest to researchers. Munjack and Moss (1981) reported that one-third of their social phobic patients had either past history or current depression. Zajecka and Ross (1995) found that as many as 70 percent of patients with social phobia or depression had the other disorder as well, with social phobia usually predating the depression. Jarrett and Schnurr (1979) found that depression is associated with social phobia and agoraphobia but not with specific phobia. The relationship between depression and social phobia is therefore well established and the evidence indicates that social phobia precedes depression in most instances. Van Amerigen et al. (1991) note that this is especially the case with patients who have a lifetime diagnosis of both: "The onset of social phobia predated the onset of major depression in 90 percent of these patients" (97). While the data on the temporal relationship of these disorders (i.e., which came first) is based on retrospective recall and should therefore be viewed with some caution, it nonetheless indicates that the vast majority of those who suffer both disorders believe that their social phobia precipitated their depression.

Heckelman and Schneier (1995) emphasize that, while this association of social phobia and depression is a strong one, they differ in their central features. While both social phobics and depressives exhibit social withdrawal and avoidance, apathy or lack of energy are likely to precipitate the avoidance behavior in depression, whereas in social phobia avoidance is associated with fear of being negatively evaluated by others. Conversely, the embarrassment that depressed patients fear in social situations occurs only during episodes of major depression, and their social fears disappear when the depression itself lifts (13–14).

Concerning the relationship of social phobia with alcohol dependence and abuse, patients typically report that social phobic symptoms came first. Heckelman and Schneier note that while alcohol sometimes provides transient relief of social phobic symptoms, it can become a costly strategy when it leads to alcohol dependence, which may then become the principal problem (16). Studies indicate a range of 16 to 36 percent of alcoholism among social phobics. Turner et al. (1986) found that roughly half of their patients made intentional use of alcohol prior to attending a social gathering or used alcohol served at the party in order to feel more sociable.

Predisposing Factors in Social Phobia

We have already considered the role that shyness plays in predisposing an individual to subsequent social phobia in adolescence and adulthood. Are there other predisposing factors? Researchers have considered a range of possible predisposing factors, including culture, race, age, gender, family of origin, parental history, and religion. To the extent that these factors play a role in placing a person at risk of social phobia, they are important diagnostic indicators.

Cultural and Racial Factors

Researchers have noted that social phobia is more prevalent in some cultures than in others. A study by Chaleby (1987) indicates that it is unusually high among males in Saudi Arabia. This is apparently because there are rigid conformist rules governing social behavior and great importance is placed on maintaining a good social reputation. Social phobia has also been of great interest in Japanese psychiatry. A feature of social phobia in Japan that has received little attention in the West is the fear that a person's social unease will make *others* uncomfortable (8). This fear tends to exacerbate anxiety in social situations. Lee and Oei (1994) found that among a number of phobic responses (reflecting specific, social, and agoraphobic conditions) their Hong Kong sample ranked speaking or performing before an audience highest, followed by being criticized, and being watched or stared at. Thus, social phobia ranked higher than the other phobias. Fears usually associated with panic or agoraphia (for example, large open spaces, traveling alone by bus or coach, walking alone in busy streets) were lowest, while various specific phobias (sight of blood, going to the dentist, etc.) fell midway between the social phobias and agoraphobia. In a comparison of Navajo and Anglo children (Tikalsky and Wallace 1988), fear was found to be greater among the Navajo children, but the authors attribute this to the fact that having many fears is generally regarded as an ominous sign in Anglo culture. In contrast, from the traditional Navajo view, having many fears is considered a sign of perceptiveness. Thus, there may be a cultural tendency for Navajos to exaggerate and for Anglos to minimize the presence of fear in their children. These processes of exaggeration and denial would not necessarily be completely conscious, and the distortion process, if it exists, may be very subtle (490). Also, the fears considered in this study were not limited to social fears. In fact, the study included a much greater number of specific (dogs, thunder, ghosts, etc.) than social phobias (reciting in class, being criticized, making mistakes, social events, making another person angry, etc.). Whether Anglo or Navajo children were more phobic on the social phobic items cannot be determined from the data the authors provided.

A study by Brown et al. (1990) found that susceptibility to phobic disorders was higher among American blacks than whites, with racial differences remaining even when socioeconomic and demographic factors like age, location, education, gender, and marital status were held constant. The authors believe that these higher rates of phobia among blacks may be due to the daily stress of marginal minority group status. However, this study did not differentiate between types of phobia and only current (not lifetime) phobias were considered.

It appears that culture and race play a significant role in predisposing an individual to social phobia, but the research in this regard is not extensive and what does exist has not produced any consistent conclusions.

Gender as a Predisposing Factor

Unlike culture and race, researchers have given a great deal of attention to gender. Chapman et al. (1995) refer to a community-based study that found higher rates of social phobia among women than men (3 percent to 2 percent lifetime), but they note that this finding does not correspond with clinically-based studies that suggest a more equal or slightly male-biased gender distribution among patients in treatment settings (29). Another study found the same 3:2 ratio of women to men with broadly defined social anxiety, but this ratio was exactly reversed (2:3) when the "significant distress" criterion of the *DSM-IV* was strictly applied. While this finding also supports the studies that indicate more men than women seek treatment for social phobia, it also raises the possibility that certain *types* of social phobia may be characterized by particular gender ratios (30).

A study by Pollard and Henderson (1988) supports this conclusion. They found that social phobias were more prevalent among women, but that speaking and performing before an audience accounted for the difference, for twice as many women than men expressed fear of public speaking or performing. The fact that this study included only three other social phobic situations (eating and writing in public and using public restrooms) may also account for the fact that public speaking and performance phobias accounted for 83 percent of the social phobias reported.

Another study by Bourdon et al. (1988) found that women had significantly higher prevalence rates for specific phobias and agoraphobia, but there were no gender differences for social phobia. Also, their findings suggested that men and women react similarly to the presence of phobia once it is established. Men and women did not show a different pattern in forgetting past episodes of the disorder or in admitting fears that are unreasonably intense and disruptive (238).

One explanation for why more men seek treatment even though more women are in fact socially phobic is that traditionally men have been expected to demonstrate the social skills associated with social phobia, including public speaking and initiating conversations. Thus, they are perhaps more likely to experience the impairing effects of social phobia. The converse may apply to the higher prevalence of agoraphobia among women, because women have traditionally been more confined to the home, especially during childbirth. In any case, social phobia is one psychopathology for which gender is not a primary predisposing factor and is therefore not relied upon by clinicians to determine whether a given individual may be a social phobic. Perhaps this is not surprising when we consider that Kagan and his colleagues found no significant gender differences in relation to behavioral inhibition or shyness. On the other hand, we should not ignore the fact that women and men may differ according to the *types* of social phobia to which they are susceptible. I will discuss the types of social phobia in greater detail in chapter 3.

Family of Origin as a Predisposing Factor

Chapman et al. (1995) note the "familial nature" of social phobia, citing studies indicating that social phobia may run in families. One study found three times as many relatives of social phobics were themselves social phobics than corresponding relatives of the control group (15 percent to 5 percent), but it also found that the disorder was more common among siblings than among parents. That is, it was far more likely that two siblings would be social phobics than that both parents would be. On the other hand, Chapman et al. note that unmarried persons are more likely than married persons to be social phobics, largely because fears of attending social gatherings, talking to strangers, and dating are all common manifestations of generalized social phobia. Thus, if social phobia runs in families, it is not as prevalent as it might otherwise be because some social phobics never marry. Also, there is the consistent finding that if social phobia is a family disorder, it is not associated with being at risk for any other anxiety disorder. In this sense, social phobia is said to "breed true," that is, it does not produce offspring susceptible to other anxiety disorders, including specific or agoraphobia. Furthermore, there is some evidence to suggest that familial transmission is more likely in the generalized than the more situation-specific forms of social phobia.

The researchers who first reported a familial influence on social phobia emphasize that the familial risk for social phobia is only moderate. While familial factors, either genetic or environmental, contribute to the development of some cases of the disorder, other nonfamilial circumstances are equally important, such as early social experiences, physical trauma, specific environmental factors, and so forth (Fyer et al. 1993, 291). They also note that while in about two-thirds of the cases relatives had some overlap in types of social phobia, none of the cases were identical, thus arguing against "exact specificity of intergenerational symptom transmission" (291).

While studies that focus on familial transmission of social phobia tend to be fueled by genetic concerns, it has proven notoriously difficult to make a convincing case that genetics are responsible for the fact that social phobias may run in families. As in the case of studies on the influence of race on social phobia, other social environmental factors as well as stressful life experiences may account for this finding of a familial influence. On the other hand, the best currently available basis for arguing that something more than social environment and stressful life experiences is involved is that social phobia has a strong association with childhood behavioral inhibition or shyness. As Bruch and Cheek (1995) point out:

> The idea that shyness is rooted in a biological predisposition is as old as the field of psychology. [William] James (1890) quoted [Charles] Darwin's discussion of shyness and included it in his list of basic human instincts. [J.M.] Baldwin (1894) also interpreted the emergence of bashfulness during the first year of life as an organic stage in the expression of instinctive emotion. Drawing on observations from his medical practice, H. Campbell (1896) argued that "no fact is more certain than that shyness runs in families." Recent work in behavior genetics tends to support these early speculations about the contribution of an inherited biological predisposition to the origins of shyness (164).

Bruch and Cheek cite several studies of identical and fraternal twins and note the conclusion of one researcher that "heredity plays a more substantial role in shyness from infancy through adulthood than it does in other personality traits (e.g., activity level and gregariousness)" (164). Thus, if studies show that family plays a predisposing role in social phobia and that this is generally through only one of the parents, behavioral inhibition or shyness may be the major pathway by which this inherited influence is acquired.

Age as a Predisposing Factor

Age of onset has been a major issue in social phobia research and treatment. As noted earlier, the fact that social phobia typically begins in adolescence, while specific phobias begin in early childhood and agoraphobia begins in young adulthood, inspired Marks and Gelder (1966) to propose that social phobia is a major type of phobia (and not merely one among a vast number of specific phobias). In one community study cited by Chapman et al. (1995) the modal category for age of onset was eleven to fifteen, indicating that age of onset tends to be in the early rather than the later adolescent years.

One consistent finding in the research literature is that specific phobias have the earliest onset, beginning in early childhood. They are usually associated with direct experience of the feared animal or object, though, in some cases, children exhibit fears on the basis of what their parents have told them. Thus, Öst (1987) reports that the phobic patient who displayed the strongest phobic reaction in his group of patients had never seen a live snake before coming to his laboratory. She ascribed the onset of her phobia to the many warnings of snakes her parents had given her during her early childhood. For specific phobias, onset was as early as four years of age. Öst found an average of 6.9 years of age in his study.

Agoraphobia typically emerges in the late teens through the mid-thirties. The *DSM-IV* suggests that there may be two peaks in the onset of agoraphobia, with one spurt occurring in late adolescence and the other in the mid-30s, though the average age of onset is 27–28 years of age.

While several studies have found a somewhat later age of onset for social phobia, adolescence is the usual period in which social phobia develops. Conversely, in cases where social phobia develops in earlier childhood, certain of the diagnostic criteria for social phobia are either irrelevant or substantially qualified, and this is not the case for social phobia that emerges in adolescence. For example, unlike the child, the adolescent is usually aware that her fear is excessive or unreasonable.

Thus, age of onset is clearly a predisposing factor, with early adolescence being the age of greatest risk for the social phobic. Age of onset, however, is only one of two important age factors. The other is the duration or prevalence of social phobia across the life span. As the *DSM-IV* indicates, an important feature of social phobia is that it is unusually persistent. Once it emerges, it tends to persist throughout life. On the other hand, a community study cited by Chapman et al. (1995) found that persons aged 18–29 had the highest lifetime rate of social phobia disorder (3.6 percent) while those aged 65 and older had the lowest rate (1.8 percent). Chapman et al. find this lower rate among older adults difficult to interpret, because it could mean that those born prior to World War II were less at risk for social phobia, a conclusion supported by evidence that rates of depressive illness in the United State's have increased over the last sixty years. However, this low rate among older adults could also mean that there is either poor recall or reduced reporting accuracy by older respondents (31). I suggest that societal biases may also be a factor, because older adults are often discouraged from speaking or performing before an audience and are often excluded from informal conversations. Thus, some of the very causes of social phobia among younger adults may not be germane to older adults, not necessarily by personal choice. For example, an elderly member of our church requested the opportunity to speak to the ushers after church one Sunday about proper decorum and dress codes. In the course of his rather agitated lecture, he suffered a stroke and died a few days later. This unfortunate episode suggests that not all efforts to discourage elderly persons from performing for an audience are merely prejudicial, but may have their own interests at heart.

Öhman's dominance/submissiveness concept, however, is relevant here, since the older adult who might otherwise experience social phobic symptoms may find that the younger adults who exercise dominance in these social settings will not allow these behaviors anyway. That is, there is an unstated but powerful assumption that older adults will assume the submissive role for the simple reason that they are older adults. Thus, older adults may find that their lifelong social phobia has been "solved" for them, not, however, because they have overcome their phobic anxieties and often at significant cost to their desire and need for sociability.

Finally, as the *DSM-IV* emphasizes, automatic remission of social phobia is rare. If it sometimes occurs, there is a likelihood that the individual's life situation has changed to such an extent that the threatening social situation is no longer part of his normal routine. Occasionally, an adult may suddenly develop a social phobia without having had a childhood history of shyness or earlier social phobic symptoms of any kind. In such cases, the prospects for remission are comparable to remission of specific phobias (i.e., much more positive). However, by and large, social phobia persists through life, which means that age cannot be used to make the judgment that an individual is *not* afflicted with social phobia. That is, social phobia is not an "adolescent disorder" that disappears once a person reaches young adulthood.

Religion as a Predisposing Factor

The relationship between religion and anxiety disorders has long been debated by mental health specialists, some arguing that religion creates or at least exacerbates anxiety, others arguing that it relieves anxiety, and still others contending that it has both effects. Yet there is very little research on the specific relationship between religion and social phobia. A recent study by Koenig et al. (1993), however, addressed the influence of religion on each of the anxiety disorders. While anxiety disorder was found to be higher among unaffiliated than affiliated young adults, there was no relationship between religious affiliation and anxiety in middle and older adults. This finding indicates a pattern of both positive and negative relationships between religion and anxiety disorder, a pattern that is most evident among adults aged 18–39, and that weakens with age. With regard to social phobia specifically, it was found that social phobia was higher among young adults with no religious affiliation (4.5 percent) than among the religiously affiliated (0.8 percent for mainline Protestants, 2.0 percent for Pentecostals, 2.9 percent for conservative Protestants). Among middle and older adults, however, social phobia was higher for the affiliated than for the unaffiliated. For middle adults, 1.1 percent of mainline Protestants, 1.7 percent of conservative Protestants, and 0.0 percent of Pentecostals were social phobics. While there were no social phobics among unaffiliated older adults, 2.3 percent of mainline Protestants, 2.6 percent of conservative Protestants, and 3.1 percent of Pentecostals were social phobics.

The authors consider this latter finding puzzling, because it suggests that the relationship between social phobia and religious affiliation has reversed itself between young and middle adulthood. Why this reversal? This finding also challenges the expectation that social phobics would be less, not more, inclined to attend church because their disorder would prohibit them from doing so. The authors suggest that religious affiliation provides other social supports that are considered sufficiently important that social phobics do not permit their phobia to inhibit their attendance. They note that the strength of the relationship between church attendance and recent anxiety disorder weakened when social support was controlled for. Thus, religious group participation may enhance social support by linking individuals to supportive interpersonal relationships. Moreover, church attendance may be a form of social integration, a way that individuals come to feel that they are part of a larger community that helps to protect against feelings of alienation and powerlessness. They suggest the possibility that the social support provided by religious group participation is, for some reason, more satisfying than other forms of support. They cite studies showing that "religious participation in particular—when compared with involvement in other secular groups or clubs—is associated with well-being" (336). Thus, the fact that there are higher rates of social phobia among the religious affiliated does not mean that religious affiliation causes social phobia. Rather, these higher rates suggest that social phobics choose affiliation with religious groups over other groups because religious groups offer more satisfying social supports.

The authors also seek to explain why younger persons with no religious affiliation had higher rates of anxiety disorder than religiously affiliated younger adults. They believe this suggests that the benefits provided younger adults by religious group participation go beyond that of providing social contacts: "Church attendance may reaffirm religious beliefs and world-view in a way that enhances cognitive—as well as social—integration and further reinforces a sense of belonging, world coherence, predictability, and safety" (336). In other words, they emphasize that the social supports provided by religious affiliation are only one aspect of a larger meaning system that alleviates anxiety among young adults.

In another study of social phobia and religious affiliation, however, Chapman et al. (1995) place particular emphasis on the social role played by religious organizations in behalf of social phobics. They point out that

> socially anxious individuals may systematically avoid informal unstructured events at which face-to-face social interaction is expected, such as parties or social gatherings, but nevertheless participate actively in less anxiety-provoking social contexts, such as church groups. All else being equal, potential spouses encountered in such settings may themselves be disproportionately likely to suffer from similar types of social anxiety (31).

While Chapman et al. do not explain why church groups might be viewed as less anxiety-provoking than parties and social gatherings, their point seems intuitively correct, for individuals are often allowed to assume a lower social profile in churches than in other social gatherings. Their point is also supported by the Koenig et al. finding that social phobia is higher among religiously affiliated middle and older adults than unaffiliated ones. Middle adults who have experienced divorce or death of a spouse and who are socially phobic may feel that religious organizations allow an easier transition to renewed social interaction than other, more intense types of social interaction (for example, parties and dates). The fact that religiously affiliated older adults had higher rates of social phobia than religiously affiliated middle adults also supports this argument, since older adults are even more likely than middle adults to be without familial social supports as a result of the loss of spouses through death, and therefore turn to the religious organization for such support.

In short, the Koenig et al. study indicates that the relationship between social phobia and religion is strongly mediated by social support. What their study does not attempt to address is the possible role of religion in *contributing* to the development of social phobia. Research studies on this issue are virtually nonexistent. This is somewhat surprising in light of the view held by William James (1982), Rudolf Otto

(1923), and Oskar Pfister (1948) that religion and fear are closely related. However, a study by Ragsdale and Durham (1966) is relevant. These researchers found that students in a basic communication course at a large southern university responded more *positively* to a religious message using high-fear appeals than one using low-fear appeals, and that the stronger the listener's religious beliefs, the more likely this positive response would be. They also found that among women (but not men listeners) there was more information retention from a high-fear message than from a low-fear message. They attribute this to the fact that the women were more religiously conservative. While this study does not deal with phobia as such, it suggests that for some religiously affiliated persons, religion is valued for its ability to *arouse* fear.

The authors do not speculate on why this would be the case, but the previous study by Koenig et al. may provide a partial answer. As Koenig et al. suggest, church attendance reinforces "a sense of belonging, world coherence, predictability, and *safety*" (336, my emphasis). If so, this could mean that religious fear appeals are valued precisely because they occur in a safe place. That is, the same fears spontaneously aroused by phobias are here aroused in a controlled situation where listeners are aware that they will be able to cope with the fear arousal. Thus a social phobic's fears may be aroused by a religious appeal but in such a way that she *cannot* be subject to negative evaluation or embarrassment because she is among the listening audience. Religion may therefore have a consoling effect, as it arouses fears but not in such a way that the phobia itself is thereby aroused.

This view that the church is a "safe place" for fear arousal receives rather unusual support from a clinical case report by Knight (1967) about a woman who suddenly developed a church phobia. One Sunday, this 37-year-old woman was listening to the minister preach on the topic of doubt. He noted that there are those who have their doubts and want proof of God. Suddenly, this thought came to her, which she addressed to God: "If you exist, strike me dead to prove it." The following Sunday she became dizzy in church and almost fainted. Her symptoms were so severe that she left during the worship service and remained away from church for nearly three years. On the few occasions she did try to attend, she could not get beyond the vestibule or had to leave before the service ended. She complained of palpitations of the heart, profuse perspiration, dizziness, and the feeling that she was going to faint.

In therapy, she attributed these symptoms to fear that God would fully accept her challenge and give her conclusive proof of his existence. To save herself from this ultimate proof, she would withdraw from the worship service when her symptoms began to develop. She reported that if a worship service was not taking place she could enter and walk anywhere in the sanctuary without getting a single symptom. When asked to explain this apparent anomaly, she answered, "I asked God to prove himself to me while a service was in progress. If God accepts my challenge, I feel that he will do so only during a church service."

What is significant about this case is the fact that her phobia developed when the worship service was suddenly altered from a safe place to a life-threatening one. Thus, this clinical case supports the view that religion may evoke the same fears that phobias evoke, but *normally* within a social/cognitive context that is safe and nonthreatening. Of course, this does not mean that ministers should deliberately engage in fear-arousing appeals as a way of "helping" phobic persons cope with their fears. As Ragsdale and Durham note, there are ethical issues here: "In the final analysis, fear appeals in sermons do have impact, leaving ministers and other Christian communicators now to wrestle with the ethical legitimacy of strong fear arousal appeals. When a minister's view is that the Christian message is a message of love, however, the question of whether to use fear appeals may simply be quite beside the point" (48).

Also, such religious appeals to fear may contribute to the development of phobias among young children. As noted earlier, Öst (1987) found that some children develop specific phobias not by direct contact with a feared object but by listening to warnings from their parents. This indicates that phobias can be created exclusively by fear-eliciting adults. To my knowledge, there are no studies that have attempted to discover the direct effects of religious communications (sermons and church school lessons) on the development of social phobias among children and adolescents. However, if a child can develop a fear of snakes without ever having seen one, it seems reasonable to assume that children may develop debilitating fears of supernatural personages and entities (a punishing God, Satan, or hell) that they know from adult testimony only. In the final chapter I will return to this issue of religion, fear, and phobic anxiety.

Parenting as a Predisposing Factor

Another possible predisposing factor is the role of negative parenting in placing a child at risk for subsequent development of social phobia. Researchers have found that phobics consistently have more negative views than nonphobics of the way they were parented. In their survey of research on this issue, Bruch and Cheek (1995) cite a study that found that, in comparison with control subjects, social phobics perceived both of their parents as more controlling and expressing less affection, while agoraphobics differed from the control group only in their perception that their mothers were less affectionate (170–171). Social phobics, especially those with generalized social phobia, also reported having experienced greater personal isolation and less family socializing during childhood. In another study (Arrindell et al. 1989), social phobics, in comparison with control subjects, rated the rearing behavior of both their parents as less consistent and as significantly lower on emotional warmth. On the other hand, they viewed their parents as more protective. This combination of less emotional warmth and greater protectiveness may create a predisposition to social phobia, as the lesser emotional warmth may cause the child to be wary around adults while the parents' message that the child needs to be protected from external dangers may make her more fearful of social situations. Another study (Bruch and Heimberg 1994) found that generalized social phobics were more likely than control subjects to believe that one or both parents isolated them and used shame to discipline them. This finding supports Buss's argument that "the most common child-rearing factor that makes one vulnerable to fear of negative evaluation is parental admonishments about inappropriate behavior. This criticism of the child stems from parents placing undue importance on the opinions of others" (1980, 165). Buss also found that social phobics were more likely to have been disciplined as children for inappropriate behavior by isolation (e.g., being sent to their bedroom) and by shaming (e.g., being told that they have let the parent down, have embarrassed their parent in front of other adults, have embarrassed themselves, etc.).

A study by Arkin (1986) suggests that high parental standards may be a factor in the development of shyness and hence of social phobia. A child who is punished when his behavior does not live up to these standards and is unrewarded when it does may acquire an abiding fear of failure. Also, consistent or anticipated rejection, coupled with reinforcement of dependence in the child, may produce anxiety and focus the child's attention on avoiding disapproval instead of seeking approval. As a result, the child may develop a protective self-presentational style, one that attends to potential losses rather than potential gains. This protective style may manifest itself in withdrawal from social interaction, the adoption of neutral or conforming attitudes, and modesty in self-evaluations as a means to self-regulate feelings of social anxiety (Arrindell et al. 1989, 526–527).

Another possible contribution to social phobia is the modeling behavior of one or both parents. Rosenbaum et al. (1991) suggest that children learn from observing fear reactions of their parents. They cite a previous study (Bruch et al. 1989) reporting that when subjects were asked to remember experiences with their parents during childhood, social phobics were more likely to recall patterns of behavior in their mothers that were reminiscent of their own socially avoidant behaviors and fears during social interaction. The Rosenbaum et al. study bears these recollections out, as the parents of social phobics had significantly higher rates of social phobia themselves. They conclude that behavioral inhibition in children may result in part from children's observations of the inhibited behaviors of one or both parents.

Another question that researchers are beginning to address is whether there is any relationship between overt parental abuse and phobia. A study by Pribor and Dinwiddie (1992) on the link between childhood incest and psychiatric disorders among women found that the rates of all anxiety disorders, including social phobia, were higher among childhood incest victims than the comparison group. Also, incest victims had an average of seven lifetime diagnoses of psychiatric illness. In the sample of 52 incest victims, 24 (or 46 percent) were diagnosed as social phobics. While depression, psychosexual dysfunction, and generalized anxiety disorder were found in substantially larger percentages of the incest victims, this study nonetheless demonstrates that victims of childhood incest are also at risk for social phobia. This finding is supported by David et al. (1995), who explored the relationship between developmental trauma and social phobia. They focused on two types of developmental trauma: physical and sexual abuse by family members, family acquaintances, and strangers; and prolonged separation from or loss of parents and/or siblings. They found that the percentages of sexual/physical abuse were about double the rate of the control group for all categories of social phobia. On the other hand, they found no difference between social phobics and the control group in regard to childhood separation from one or both parents or loss of a parent. They also suggest that being a shy or anxious child increases the risk of experiencing parental abuse, as a parent is more likely to take advantage of an inhibited child (116). The fact that no relationship was found between social phobia and parental loss or prolonged separation makes the finding of a link between physical and sexual abuse and social phobia all the more significant.

Researchers emphasize that much of the evidence supporting a relationship between social phobia and negative parenting is based on retrospective accounts. Thus, they recommend treating these findings with caution. As Rosenbaum et al. (1991) point out, "Theories implicating parent-child interaction in the etiology of social phobia rely heavily on retrospective self-report information, which may be biased by the parents' current emotional state" (11). These retrospective reports may also be influenced by social phobics' own theories as to how they became socially phobic. Thus, they may attribute their phobia to one or both parents when the situation itself is far more complex. For example, emphasis placed exclusively on the mother-child dyad overlooks other familial interactions and relationships, including not only father-child relationships but also sibling relationships.

Rapee's (1995) descriptive account of the psychopathology of social phobia provides another basis for caution concerning retrospective self-reports. He notes that social phobics tend to interpret "ambiguous feed-back" more negatively than other subjects do (52). If this finding is applied to their retrospective view of parental treatment, this could mean that as children they tended to interpret "neutral" behavior by parents as negative. Since social phobics are unusually sensitive to negative judgments by others, this sensitivity may also apply to their retrospective impressions of how they were viewed and treated by their parents. This argument does not apply to overt physical and sexual abuse, since there is nothing "ambiguous" about overt abuse. But it would apply to impressions that their parents were emotionally cold or distant, were more likely to be concerned about public opinion, were more likely to use shaming methods, and so forth. What the adult social phobic recalls as "emotional coldness" may be remembered by one of his siblings as the absence of emotional affect and therefore not inherently negative. What are needed are sibling studies comparable to the twinship studies employed in genetic research in order to explore this issue of retrospective recall in greater depth.

Conclusion

In this chapter, I have considered the criteria used to make a diagnosis of social phobia and have discussed various factors that predispose a person to become socially phobic. Regarding the predisposing factors, we should keep in mind that the most often cited predisposing factor in the literature is shyness, the factor discussed in the preceding chapter. This does not, however, mean that the other predisposing factors are unimportant, for social phobia is an anxiety disorder that is experienced very differently by the persons who suffer from it. These nonbiological predisposing factors may account for such experiential differences. I will return in chapter 7 to the issue of cultural influences and in chapter 8 to the issue of religion. Thus far we have seen that culture has some influence on the ways in which social phobia is experienced and interpreted, and we have also seen that religion has a rather complex relationship to social phobia, since it may, on the one hand, exacerbate social phobic symptoms and, on the other hand, alleviate them. In the cases of culture and religion, however, we have only begun to scratch the surface of their respective roles in social phobia. More penetrating analyses must be set aside for now as we explore the types and severity of phobic situations in chapter 3 and therapeutic methods in chapters 4–6.

Types and Severity of Phobic Situations

Thus far we have discussed the criteria used for identifying persons who are socially phobic, and we have explored some of the most important factors that predispose a person to become socially phobic. In this chapter, I consider in greater detail the types of social situations that social phobics most fear and the severity of anxiety or fear attached to these situations.

What are the social situations that social phobics tend most to fear and to avoid? Unlike hostage victims, social phobics do not live in a general state of heightened anxiety. Rather, they experience anxiety as they anticipate or dread the very thought of their presence or involvement in specific social situations. Over the past several decades, researchers and clinicians have tried to find out what types of social situations are feared and avoided by social phobics. They have also tried to determine which of these situations are most feared and avoided.

In a study based on 160 subjects, Rapee et al. (1988) presented subjects with a list of nine situations known to be ones that social phobics fear. They wanted to ascertain whether subjects had slight or moderate fear of the situation in question and whether their degree of avoidance of this situation was slight or moderate. Sixty-three percent were men, 37 percent women. Their mean age was 33, and the mean number of years they had been diagnosed as socially phobic was 21 years. The table that I have constructed from their findings for social phobics is presented on the following page.

TABLE 1
Percentage of Social Phobics Reporting Fear and Avoidance
in Various Social Situations

Social Situation	Slight Fear	Moderate Fear	Slight Avoid	Moderate Avoid
Public speaking	97%	91%	91%	77%
Meetings	91%	68%	68%	38%
Parties	89%	67%	71%	59%
Talking to authorities	83%	69%	77%	50%
Asserting oneself	71%	40%	68%	38%
Dating	57%	48%	48%	39%
Writing in public	38%	15%	19%	13%
Using public restrooms	31%	23%	27%	18%
Eating in public	26%	14%	24%	15%

This table indicates that public speaking is the most feared and avoided social situation. Attending meetings is the second most feared, but is only the fourth or fifth most avoided, apparently because many meetings are not considered avoidable. One may choose not to attend a party, go out on a date, or speak to someone in authority but feel that attendance at a scheduled meeting is required. It should also be noted that types of social phobia emphasized in the early literature (eating and writing in public and using a public restroom) are not as feared or avoided as speaking with persons in authority and asserting oneself. This supports the view that social phobics are unusually reactive to the dominance/submissiveness system in social contexts.

While the terms "slight" and "moderate" may imply that subjects were not highly fearful or avoidant of these situations, this is not the case, as the researchers found that the average number of situations that social phobics feared was five and the average number of situations avoided was four. This means that their social phobia has considerable influence over their daily routines. Also, comparisons between the social phobics and persons with other phobias indicate that social phobics scored much higher on fear and avoidance of these social situations than did the other phobics. For example, while 91 percent of social phobics experience at least moderate fear of public speaking, only 56 percent of agoraphobics and 50 percent of specific phobics did so. In contrast to social phobics, 68 percent of whom had moderate fear of meetings, only 23 percent of agoraphobics had moderate fear of meetings, and none of the specific phobics did so. Very substantial differences between social phobics and the other phobic types were also found for fear and avoidance of speaking with persons in authority. However, on one social phobia measure—eating in public—agoraphobics experienced greater fear and avoidance, and they were nearly equal to social phobics in fear and avoidance of writing in public. Again, this suggests that some of the more traditional situations of social phobia are less discriminating for social phobia than more recently identified ones (such as speaking to an authority figure and asserting oneself).

The general picture that this study offers of social phobics is that they fear and avoid situations in which they are expected to speak before an audience, to speak to persons in authority, and to attend meetings and other social gatherings where they may be expected to participate verbally or speak informally. The common feature appears to be that of verbal communication. This feature has some clear predisposing characteristics in the fact that shy or behaviorally-inhibited children tend to speak in a lower, more subdued, or halting voice than other children. A second related theme is that social phobics fear being self-assertive and much prefer to assume a neutral, even submissive role in most social contexts. Thus, these rankings of feared and avoided social situations support the view (Arrindell et al. 1989) that social phobics develop a protective self-presentational style, one that manifests itself through withdrawal from social interaction, the adoption of neutral or conforming attitudes, and modesty in self-attribution as a means to self-regulate feelings of social anxiety.

Another study (Holt et al. 1992) develops the concept of *situational domains* to investigate the pervasiveness of social phobia among similar situations. Four conceptually different situational domains were defined on the basis of previous research: (1) formal speaking and interaction; (2) informal speaking and interaction; (3) observation by others; and (4) assertion. The authors note, for example, that public speaking and reporting at a meeting are conceptually similar instances of formal interaction and may therefore be considered variations of the same type of social situation. They decided to report only their findings on anxiety or fear arousal and not, as in the previous study by Rapee et al., avoidance behavior. This decision was based on doubts concerning the meaning of avoidance ratings from self-report or clinical interviews because of the difficulty of determining whether an individual is actively avoiding a situation or simply has a lifestyle in which these situations do not present themselves. A summary of the four situational domains and the anxiety/fear ratings given the individual items is provided in table 2. There were three anxiety/fear ratings: mild, moderate, and severe. Ninety-one persons were studied.

The results indicate that the formal speaking and interaction domain had the highest percentage of anxiety/fear arousal across the three severity rankings (mild, moderate, severe).

TABLE 2
Social Situational Domains and Percent of Sample
With Mild, Moderate, and Severe Anxiety/Fear Ratings

Situational Domain Social Phobia Scale Items	% Mild	% Moderate	% Severe
Formal speaking and interaction			
Acting, performing, or giving a talk in front of an audience	93	86	71
Giving a report to a group	91	81	59
Speaking up at a meeting	92	76	51
Participating in small groups	84	56	26
Informal speaking and interaction			
Trying to pick up someone	85	73	43
Going to a party	85	63	30
Giving a party	82	58	34
Meeting strangers	74	47	15
Calling someone you don't know very well	67	39	12
Assertive interaction			
Talking to people in authority	85	61	23
Expressing a disagreement or disapproval to people you don't know very well	80	55	19
Returning goods to a store	58	33	6
Resisting a high pressure salesperson	48	23	10
Observation of behavior			
Working while being observed	79	56	30
Writing while being observed	53	36	14
Eating in public places	43	25	11
Drinking in public places	41	13	11

They also show, however, that there was at least one anxiety/fear arousal situation in each of the four domains that created anxiety/fear among a high percentage of the persons studied. For example, in the situational domain of informal speaking and interaction, 85 percent experienced at least mild anxiety when trying to pick up someone or when going to a party. The same high percentage occurred in the assertive interaction domain for talking to people in authority. Working while being observed was especially anxiety/fear arousing in the situational domain of observation of behavior. Also, because this study includes "severe" anxiety/fear, it gives a stronger indication than the Rapee et al. study that subjects found many of these situations to be extremely threatening. fifty percent or more experienced severe anxiety/fear arousal in performing before an audience, giving a report to a group, or speaking up at a meeting.

The authors also tested to see whether individuals experienced "full involvement" in a situational domain (defined as anxiety/fear arousal on all but one of the items in a given domain). These results were cross-tabulated with the three intensity levels (mild, moderate, and severe). They found that 90 percent of the subjects were fully involved in the formal domain, 69 percent in the informal domain, 60 percent in the assertion domain, and 40 percent in the observation domain. When mild scores were excluded and only moderate and severe scores were retained, these percentages dropped to 70 percent, 46 percent, 31 percent, and 22 percent, and when only severe scores were retained, the percentages dropped to 51 percent, 11 percent, 4 percent, and 10 percent. The authors conclude that social phobics are likely to be anxious about several situations in a situational domain. Also, by using the threshold of moderate anxiety, about 80 percent of the sample could be classified within at least one of the domains. When the less rigorous criterion of mild anxiety was used, too many of the subjects could be classified within several domains, thus reducing the diagnostic power of the situational domain concept. Conversely, when the more rigorous criterion of severe anxiety was used, many subjects experienced severe anxiety over only one item in a situational domain. The authors therefore recommend the use of moderate anxiety as the most useful diagnostic threshold. It enables the clinician to assign individual patients to a primary situational domain.

While the results of this study are consistent with Rapee et al.'s finding that performing before an audience or group elicits the greatest amount of anxiety, and that eating and drinking in public are among the least anxiety arousing, it also shows that individuals tend to have anxieties that are domain specific. This does not mean that a person who is a formal speaking and interaction phobic may not also have fears associated with situations in other domains, but it does mean that these four domains effectively identify social phobics according to types, and thus enable us to differentiate social phobia accordingly.

The Protective Self-representational Style of Social Phobics

A major issue in the study of social phobics is how they have learned to cope with their disability. Since social phobics do not manifest the more pronounced or extreme isolative behaviors of avoidant personality

disorder, the fact that they suffer from an anxiety disorder is not immediately self-evident to the persons with whom they associate and may
not even be evident to themselves. Furthermore, the vast majority of
social phobics never seek treatment for this disability, and many are
diagnosed as such when they seek treatment for some other problem.
We may therefore assume that in order to cope with their untreated or
unrecognized disorder, social phobics have developed coping strategies to alleviate some of the anxiety they experience in certain social
situations.

One coping strategy is avoidance of such situations altogether. Since
social phobia typically begins in early adolescence, before most persons have decided on a career choice, we may assume that some social
phobics avoid anxiety-arousing situations by choosing careers in which
these situations are unlikely (or perceived to be unlikely) to occur. Another way that social phobics avoid threatening social situations, such
as parties and dates, is to offer rationalizations or excuses for turning
invitations down. Social phobics can become quite adept in finding plausible explanations for why they cannot attend various social functions.
A social phobic of my acquaintance often pleads the death of a relative,
then worries that someone may recognize that he has used the passing
of his grandmother more times than is biologically possible. Also, the
relationship cannot be so intimate that his excuses will elicit strong expressions of sympathy and condolence, yet must be close enough that
it would seem plausible that he could find a pleasurable night out to be
demeaning to the deceased person's memory.

The coping strategies that most interest researchers and clinicians,
however, are those employed to get one through a dreaded social
situation. What strategies do social phobics use in order to survive
unavoidable social situations? Clinicians are especially interested in such
coping strategies as alcohol or other self-medication prior to or during
the dreaded social event, but researchers and clinicians are also intrigued
by the more subtle behaviors of which they may not be consciously
aware because such behaviors have become habitual over time.

One of the most enlightening theories about the coping behaviors
of social phobics is that they tend to develop a protective self-
representational style so as to minimize the possible damage of feared
social situations on their self-image and social-image. As noted earlier,
while this protective self-representational style may be reflected in actual
avoidance of social interaction, it also involves the adoption of neutral
or conforming attitudes in social situations and a deliberate modesty in
self-attribution so as to avoid being the center of attention (Arrindell et
al. 1989).

A recent study (Wells et al. 1995) on the safety behaviors of social phobics further clarifies how they use neutral or conforming attitudes in unavoidable social situations. These authors wanted to address the rather puzzling fact that patients do not experience a marked reduction in anxiety merely by being exposed to anxiety-eliciting social situations. In contrast to patients with specific phobias and many agoraphobics, exposure to the feared situation as a treatment method has resulted in only modest or negligible improvement among social phobics. Why is this? One explanation is that "several mechanisms prevent exposure from providing patients with unambiguous disconfirmation of their fears" (153). The authors cite a study (Salkoviskis 1991) indicating that in-situation safety behaviors play an important role in the maintenance of anxiety because they prevent a person from experiencing an unambiguous disconfirmation of her unrealistic beliefs about feared catastrophes. When safety behaviors are used, the phobic person tends to attribute the nonoccurrence of feared catastrophes to the implementation of the safety behavior. Another study cited by Wells et al. (Stopa & Clark 1993) found that in some feared situations, individuals with social phobia behave in a less friendly and outgoing fashion than nonphobic persons. These are safety behaviors that tend to confirm his belief that he is being negatively evaluated by others because most people tend to dislike unfriendly or even neutral social behavior. Cognitive-behavioral treatment programs often involve teaching socially phobic persons conversational skills and other coping strategies to improve their social behavior. While these can be helpful, they may become safety behaviors, protecting social phobics from experiencing unambiguous disconfirmation of their negative beliefs. For example, asking other people about themselves is a good way to promote conversation, but it becomes problematic if phobic persons mainly use it as a means to protect themselves from being the focus of attention (159). The authors recommend a treatment plan in which social phobics are encouraged to divest themselves of their customary safety behaviors so that they are deprived of their usual explanation for why the feared catastrophe did not occur.

Another study on the protective self-representational style of social phobics (Leary and Kowalski 1995) supports the view that therapeutic efforts to improve social phobics' conversational skills may be counterproductive. The authors point out that persons who are low in social anxiety attempt to convey a favorable image of themselves to others, whereas socially anxious persons have a low expectancy of sustaining a positive image of themselves in the eyes of others and therefore adopt a protective self-presentational strategy aimed at minimizing social losses. When persons doubt that they will make the impressions they desire, the safest tactic is often to disaffiliate, either by remaining quietly present or by leaving the situation altogether. Such tactics allow them to avoid further damage to their social images (106). Also, when people who doubt their ability to make desired impressions remain in a social encounter, they tend to engage in relatively safe interpersonal behaviors, ones that allow them to remain at least minimally engaged while protecting their social image (106). For example, socially anxious people tend to be innocuously sociable—smiling and nodding frequently and using a high number of acknowledgments to indicate that they are attentive to the conversation ("uh-huh"). They also tend to ask more questions, a low-risk tactic that conveys friendly interest while keeping attention off oneself. They make fewer statements of fact or opinion, thus evoking fewer rebuttals. Such behaviors are useful ways of remaining engaged in an interaction without risking damage to one's image, and they help to keep the spotlight off oneself (106).

Leary and Kowalski also note that protective self-representation can be seen in the attributions that socially anxious persons make. Unlike nonsocially anxious persons who exhibit a self-serving bias by taking credit for success while denying responsibility for failure, socially anxious persons tend to reverse this self-serving bias. They are careful not to present overly self-aggrandizing images of themselves that might lead to scoffing, criticism, or rejection. While some researchers have argued that these self-protective behaviors reflect actual deficits in social skills, others have contended that they require considerable interpersonal ability. Thus, Trower and Gilbert (1989) suggest that socially anxious submissive behaviors may be a response to the accurate perception that social evaluation is in fact taking place. Rather than reflecting a social skills deficit, these behaviors are intentionally enacted to avoid negative evaluation by other people (107). This suggestion supports the view, articulated by Öhman, that social phobics are unusually sensitive to dominance/submissiveness dynamics in social interactions. They have become highly skilled in protecting themselves from the negative judgment of the dominant group in any given social situation.

But why are social phobics so predisposed to believe that they will not make a good impression if they abandon their self-protective demeanor and assume a more central or dominant position in a social situation? Studies show that this belief is not supported by the facts, for social phobics are not inherently inferior to those who assume more dominant positions in social situations. For example, with respect to academic performance, social phobics are no different from nonanxious individuals in overall educational attainment or school grades. Yet social phobics usually do not contribute to classroom and seminar discussions (Rapee, 1995, 48). With regard to social skills, the evidence is somewhat mixed. While it is true that social phobics sometimes do not perform as well as others in social situations, this is not because they do not know what makes for good social performance. They simply cannot act on this knowledge because their anxiety is inhibiting.

One explanation for phobics' resistance to evidence that they can compete successfully with others in social situations is that they have higher standards for what constitutes a good performance (Leary and Kowalski 1995, 107). This may also explain why social phobics tend to rate their own performances more negatively than independent judges rate these same performances. It also helps to explain the related fact that social phobics and nonphobics are equally accurate in rating other persons' performances (Rapee & Lim 1992; Rapee 1995, 52–53). This means that they possess the requisite skills to make judgments about social performance. Yet with regard to their own performance, they are typically hypercritical and are likely to give disproportionate attention to the one or two minor mistakes or flaws in their performance. As Hope et al. (1990) point out, one or two speech dysfluencies are much more salient to the social phobic than five minutes of fluent speech. Why? Because the dysfluencies are consistent with the social phobic's self-schemata and are therefore more extensively processed and remembered. Thus, the social phobic reports that the dysfluencies are characteristic of her verbal behavior while others are likely to see fluency as more characteristic. As a result, the social phobic's self-concept as a poor social interactor is confirmed, in spite of evidence to the contrary (185). This belief that they actually do perform poorly even though objective observers may disagree is one basis for researchers' conclusion that social phobics are unnecessarily apprehensive about the negative judgments of others.

However, the unusually high standards that social phobics hold for themselves are also important. As we saw earlier, social phobics recall that their parents were critical of their behavior as children and that they used shaming methods a great deal in the effort to correct and improve their child's behavior. The social phobic's high personal standards regarding social performance may reflect the internalization of these parental criticisms. In effect, social phobics avoid opportunities to speak or perform before audiences not only because they have *unreasonable* fears that they will be judged negatively by *others*, but also because they have *reasonable* fears that they will be negatively judged by *themselves*. If they avoid a social performance, they also avoid this negative self-criticism. This conclusion is supported by recent literature on shame that indicates that whereas guilt is the experience of not meeting the expectations of others, shame is the experience of not living up to one's own expectations or standards (Kaufman 1985; Morrison 1996).

This suggests that while social phobics may feel self-conscious in social situations because they are being scrutinized by others, their self-consciousness is also due to being the object of their own scrutiny. As paradoxical as this possibility may seem, it is supported by the consistent finding that social phobics engage in an excessive amount of "self-focused attention" (Clark & Wells 1995, 82). For persons who are unusually worried about what others think of them, it may seem odd that they are so self-focused, even to the extent of inaccurately processing external clues regarding themselves. This is not odd, however, if we assume that they experience themselves as much the object of their own negative scrutiny as they are of the negative scrutiny of others. Support for this view is provided by Lindeman's observation that "the cognitive component of social phobia involves worry both over the public embarrassment and the private shame of not meeting the demands of the situation." Also, in social phobia, "a negative evaluation is generalized to the entire personhood" (1994, 166). Lindeman's reference to "private shame" and his observation that the negative evaluation is generalized to the "entire personhood" of the social phobic is consistent with the theory that the total self is implicated in shame experiences. As Lynd points out: "Shame is an experience that affects and is affected by the whole self. Separate, discrete acts or incidents, including those seemingly most trivial, have importance because in this moment of *self-consciousness*, the self stands revealed. The thing that has been exposed is what I am" (1958, 49–50).

Of course, this does not mean that social phobics are oblivious to the effect that they have on others or that they are unconcerned about others' negative judgments of them. Nor does it mean that the safety behaviors they adopt are only for the purpose of avoiding situations in which they shame themselves. After all, the personal shame that social phobics experience is shame that occurs in a social setting, which distinguishes them from individuals whose shame is related to private behaviors (for example, autoeroticism, binge eating, and so forth). Therefore, social phobics are highly sensitive to how others may be perceiving them, and their safety behaviors are meant to enable them to maintain whatever positive impressions others may already have of them. On the other hand, social phobics tend to disbelieve that these impressions may actually be enhanced by social interaction. This implies that social phobics have a related belief that whatever may be the basis for any positive impression that others have of them is due to their accomplishments outside of social interaction (e.g., a student's ability to write excellent term papers or an employee's ability to complete a vast amount of paperwork). This means that social phobics tend to rely heavily on their nonsocial skills in order to nurture and maintain a positive social image. Their safety behaviors in unavoidable social situations serve the purpose of maintaining this social image. "Losing face" is what concerns them. They rarely consider the possibility that they might "gain face" from their performance in social situations.

Researchers and clinicians believe that social phobics are therefore too conservative in their expectations of social situations. Social phobics are unnecessarily disbelieving that something positive might come from the social situations in which they engage. If something positive should occur, they believe it will be because someone else draws attention to their achievements (e.g., a professor praising a student's work before the entire class) and not because they might enhance their image through their own social performance. Disconfirmation of this negative belief may depend on the abandonment of safety behaviors and allowing the social situation to become more fluid, more productive of unexpected occurrences and outcomes. For example, if the social phobic abandons his "innocuous sociability" and expresses an opinion, others may respond favorably, and he will experience the social encounter as a positive, even exhilarating event. The anxiety normally experienced is likely to dissipate during such moments. Thus, researchers and clinicians who view safety behaviors as a major reason for the persistence of social phobia do not believe that mere exposure to feared situations will do much good. What the social phobic needs to do is to relinquish one or more safety behaviors and allow the situation to take care of itself. This means, however, that she is being asked to trust the situation when it has been her natural disposition to mistrust it. Why social phobics mistrust certain situations is an important question, one that takes us back to the issue of the dominance/submissiveness dynamic in social contexts.

Social Phobics' Mistrust of Social Situations

As the Holt et al. (1992) study of situational domains indicates, "assertive interaction" is one of the four major situational domains that cause social phobics to experience anxiety. The items listed under this category include: talking to people in authority, expressing a disagreement or disapproval to persons one does not know very well, returning goods to a store, and resisting a high-pressure salesperson. The fact that in this situational domain, talking to people in authority and expressing disagreement or disapproval, were the items that caused social phobics the greatest amount of discomfort suggests that this situational domain taps into the dominance/submissiveness system of the social order. The first of these behaviors involves direct communication with dominant persons in the social order and the second involves abandoning one's customary position of submission and assuming a dominant position. The other two items may also be interpreted in dominance/submissiveness terms, for when a person returns goods to a store, this often means that he places himself in the position of being dominated by another by having to explain why he has changed his mind; and the high-pressure salesperson places the social phobic in a submissive situation over which he has limited control. In other words, social phobics tend to fear situations in which the dominance/submissiveness system becomes fluid or unpredictable, either because they are being expected to become more dominant or because they are being forced to become even more submissive than they normally tend to be. Any assertive act on their part tends to change the dominance/submissiveness equation. Thus, they view such assertive acts with a great deal of anticipatory anxiety. Conversely, however, situations in which they are made to feel more submissive than usual are also anxiety eliciting. They would like to remove themselves from such situations but lack the behavorial repertoire for doing so (e.g., demanding that the salesperson take the item back or desist from his high-pressure tactics).

In their assessment of Öhman's theory of the role of dominance/submissiveness dynamics in social phobia, Mineka and Zinbarg (1995) add to its complexity by citing animal studies involving social defeat. They make three related points. One is that among various animal species, repeated defeat leads to an increase in submissive behavior and a lowering of position in a dominance hierarchy, whereas repeated victory leads to an increase in aggressiveness and a rise in position in a dominance hierarchy. Repeated defeat also leads to a greater reluctance to defend oneself actively. These authors suggest that animals' timidity in retaliating when attacked provides a "close analogue" to the lack of assertiveness associated with social phobia (150). Thus, while the social phobic's mistrust of the social situation may be excessive or unreasonable, she very likely has a history of social defeats. Her safety behaviors are therefore designed to forestall or hold future social defeats to a minimum. The innocuous sociability of the social phobic functions to maintain the dominance/submissiveness status quo because, in the social phobic's view, any changes in the status quo are likely to result in still another social defeat.

Mineka and Zinbarg's second point is that defeated animals are not only submissive to the specific animals who have defeated them in the past, but are also submissive in response to the general deportment of any aggressive animal (150–151). Thus, even if an aggressive-appearing animal has not directly threatened them, they take no chances, assuming a submissive position in order to forestall any future act of aggression. This situation also offers a close analogue to social phobia because it is rare that social phobics are frightened only of a specific person. Rather, they are most often afraid of classes of people, such as strangers or people in authority. Thus, when social phobics disbelieve assurances that they have nothing to fear from a given social situation, this is because they perceive that a whole class of persons is poised to threaten them. And who are these persons? They are the group that she perceives to be dominant in the social situation. Because social phobics are fearful of a class of persons, they tend not to have personal feeling toward particular individuals in authority positions. Instead, they mistrust authority persons in general. For example, a social phobic may claim that he has nothing against the current manager of the firm he works for, but that he mistrusts managers in general. Also, he may have a good personal relationship with the manager outside the firm, yet mistrust this same individual in social interactions within the firm.

Mineka and Zinbarg make a third point that is relevant to the dominance/submissiveness issue for social phobics. This is that perceptions of control over stressful situations moderate the experience of social anxiety in animals (151). They note studies showing that if animals have a means of escape from a stressful situation, they have considerably fewer negative physiological symptoms. Such studies are relevant to social phobia in humans because they help to explain why social phobics associate having some control in a stressful situation with "escape learning" (153–154). Of course, escape learning is the opposite of assertiveness. For the social phobic, however, it is one means of control in a situation in which she assumes that the submissive position is her only option. By leaving the situation altogether (e.g., wordlessly walking away from the high-pressure salesperson), the social phobic avoids social defeat at the hands of the dominant group.

By drawing attention to how the dominance/submissiveness system is perceived by social phobics, my point is not to justify the social phobic's position. The fact that social phobics have a fear that is "excessive or unreasonable" (as *DSM-IV* puts it) is not one that I would want to contest. However, social phobics are typically able to point to one or more experiences in the past in which they suffered social defeat, so their negative beliefs about certain social situations have some basis in fact. Also, while the nonassertiveness of the social phobic is a major part of the problem and therefore needs to be counteracted, we should also recognize that this behavior has its basis in the belief that the social phobic will never become a member of the dominant class in social situations, a belief that is not entirely misguided, especially if we consider that many social phobics are temperamentally shy.

Thus, merely encouraging a social phobic to be more assertive in social situations is unlikely to produce significant change. Yet it can be helpful to encourage social phobics to engage in assertive behaviors that do not challenge the dominance/submissiveness status quo in social situations. In their study of the structure of assertiveness, Arrindell et al. (1989) suggest that there are four types of assertiveness that socially phobic persons typically avoid. The first is the display of negative feelings. This may include requesting a change in another person's irritating behavior, standing up for one's rights in a public situation, taking the initiative to resolve a social problem (e.g., requesting another table at a restaurant), and refusing the requests of others. The second is expression of and dealing with personal limitations. This may include admitting ignorance about a topic of discussion, the ability to accept and deal with criticism from others, and requesting help and attention. The third is initiating assertiveness, especially in expressing one's own opinion on a topic under discussion. The fourth is praising others and the ability to deal with compliments and praise. This includes the expression of positive feelings regarding another person's social performance and learning to accept the praise of another without responding with self-deprecatory comments.

This is a useful construct because it enables the social phobic to identify which types of assertiveness may arouse the least anxiety (i.e., the least threat to the dominance/submissiveness status quo) and it encourages him to begin his efforts to be more assertive with these. In making this suggestion, however, I have begun to anticipate the concerns of the next three chapters, which focus on the types of therapy that have been employed with socially phobic individuals.

Conclusion

In this chapter I have been concerned with the types and severity of social situations conducive to social phobia. I have suggested that the most useful typologies are those that identify situational domains rather than discrete or singular phobic situations. Ever since Marks and Gelder proposed in 1966 that social phobia is one of three major types of phobia, there has been a steady movement away from viewing social phobias in the same manner that specific phobias are viewed (i.e., as concerning a single feared object or situation) and toward viewing them as involving situational domains. By viewing them in this manner, there is increased likelihood of discovering the underlying reasons why an individual experiences anxiety in certain social situations and not in others.

I have also considered the protective self-representational style of the social phobic. This has enabled us to explore the typical ways in which social phobics present themselves to others in anxiety-arousing situations. Thus comparisons are possible between the ways a social phobic presents herself in feared situations versus the ways she presents herself in social situations that do not elicit anxiety or fear. The difference between the two is a useful measure of the scope and degree of distress experienced by a socially phobic individual. In the course of my discussion of this topic, I have explored once again the dominance/submissiveness issue because it enables us to raise questions concerning the degree to which social phobia is pathological versus the degree to which it is an adaptive response, especially in light of the fact that many social phobics are temperamentally shy and behaviorally inhibited, which normally excludes them from the dominant class in many social situations. This issue has direct bearing on the therapeutic concerns of the next three chapters and on the cultural matters to be discussed in chapter 7.

CHAPTER 4

Traditional Treatment Methods

In this chapter I will discuss the treatment approaches that were especially prominent in the first two decades following Marks and Gelder's official identification in 1966 of social phobia as a major phobia type. That these treatment methods were developed early does not mean that they are now obsolete. They continue to have their own practitioners, and each has been incorporated into newer treatment programs.

Before I discuss these more established therapeutic methods, however, I want to comment briefly on a problem to which I alluded in the introduction, that few social phobics actually seek treatment. In a study of a sample of the general United States population (Pollard et al. 1989), 142 individuals were diagnosed as having agoraphobia, social phobia, or obsessive-compulsive disorder. They were asked if and where they sought professional help and how they found treatment for their problem. While 40 percent of the agoraphobics and 28 percent of the obsessive-compulsives sought professional help, only 8 percent of the social phobics reported having sought professional help, and almost half of these had not seen a mental health professional. This unusually low rate of treatment seeking prompts us to wonder if there is something unique about social phobics' failure to seek assistance. Presumably, they are no less aware of the availability of treatment than are agoraphobics and obsessive-compulsive persons.

One very plausible explanation is that social phobics find the very act of seeking treatment more anxiety arousing than do persons suffering from other phobias. To seek treatment means that one is voluntarily entering a social situation involving conversation with a stranger. This alone may be enough to dissuade a social phobic from seeking help. Also, because the other person in this context is the "professional" and the treatment seeker is the "patient" or "client," this situation may evoke anxieties relating to the dominance/submissiveness dynamics in social interaction. The anxiety level that a social phobic might experience in this case could be comparable to that experienced in speaking to other persons in authority.

Another intriguing research finding having possible bearing on this issue is that many social phobics dislike talking on the phone. Jansen et al. (1994) identify the inability to initiate or answer a telephone call as a social phobia because it involves social interaction. In their view, it is not a specific phobia because the telephone is a social instrument. There may be as much anticipatory anxiety before a dreaded phone call as before a direct social interaction. In an exchange of letters published in the *American Journal of Psychiatry* (April 1995), a journal reader criticized the methodology of a study of social phobia in the previous issue because the authors had used telephone interviews to assess the level of social anxiety in the community being studied. The letter writer cited two earlier studies indicating that one of the primary situations avoided by social phobics is using the telephone. He concluded: "Although one cannot know the extent to which socially phobic individuals were excluded, it is clear that because of their tendency to avoid telephones, social phobia subjects were underrepresented in this study. It is like interviewing people at the top of the Empire State Building to estimate the prevalence of acrophobia [i.e., fear of heights]. One simply cannot obtain accurate measures in this way" (Kessler 1995, 653).

In their reply, the original authors (Stein et al. 1995) wrote that they "agree with Kessler that *some* social phobia subjects may avoid answering the telephone, although we would submit that it is not true for *most* social phobic subjects. In our clinical experience, although it is true that approximately 50 percent of generalized social phobia subjects often avoid *initiating* a telephone conversation, avoidance around *answering* the telephone occurs in less than one-third of such individuals" (653). In a sense, however, this reply *confirms* the letter writer's point. For interview purposes, social phobics are possibly underestimated by somewhat less than one third, a very sizeable minority. But even more significantly, their response suggests that as many as half of all social phobics might not seek treatment because they are too anxious to initiate the necessary phone call that seeking treatment normally requires. Thus, social phobia involves the curious but very real paradox that inability to seek treatment is one of the symptoms of the disorder. As Akillas and Efran (1995) observe, almost half of the students who initially expressed interest in participating in a treatment and study project on social phobia decided not to participate after all. They note: "The recruitment of socially anxious individuals is complicated by the very nature of their problems. Many such individuals express interest in participating but then attempt to postpone their involvement, claiming schedule pressures and various other exigencies. Reports of workers at Temple University's Social Anxiety Project indicate that many of these individuals experience a severe approach-avoidance conflict when facing the actual possibility of participation in treatment" (266). Note that inaccurate or false reasons were given for withdrawing from the project, indicating that many social phobics have difficulty speaking directly about their problem even when the person spoken to is known to be aware of it.

On the other hand, some social phobics do voluntarily seek treatment, and others are diagnosed as being social phobics when they seek professional help for other problems. As a result, there is now a substantial clinical literature describing the procedures that have been used in the treatment of social phobics and a smaller but growing research literature on the relative success rates of these various methods. I will focus in this and the two following chapters only on the most widely used treatment methods, and I will not discuss the pharmacological treatments (e.g., the use of beta blockers, monoamine oxibase inhibitors, benzodiaphrines, etc.) that have been used with socially anxious patients. For readers interested in these methods, Potts and Davidson (1995) provide an excellent review of pharmacological treatments and their effectiveness. Instead I will focus on the psychological treatments for social phobia. Yet even here one needs to be selective because there are many such treatment methods. In their survey of psychological methods for the treatment of social phobia, Heimberg and Barlow (1988) identify the following: systematic desensitization, social skills training, imaginal flooding, applied progressive relaxation training, graduated exposure, anxiety management training, and a variety of cognitive restructuring procedures (self-instructional training, rational-emotive therapy, and cognitive-behavioral group therapy). While I cannot discuss all of these methods in depth, I will consider a representative number of them, thereby providing a broad overview of how therapy with social phobics is currently conducted.

The treatment methods that I will discuss in this chapter include graduated exposure, social skills training, behavioral treatment, and self-efficacy treatment. Not all of these precisely fit Heimberg and Barlow's classification, but each is representative of the primary treatment methods used in the first two decades of clinical work with social phobics. Some of these methods, with modifications, are still being used, while in the case of others, their basic insights have been incorporated into newer, more inclusive methods.

The Exposure Method of Treatment

The exposure method was one of the earlier developed treatment methods for all types of phobias. This method exposes the individual to the feared situation on a repeated, prolonged, and graduated basis. Each successive exposure needs to provoke symptoms of anxiety, and the procedure is considered ineffective if the patient is insufficiently "engaged" in the exposure experience. Merely placing the patient in the feared situation is not enough. Her anxiety must be aroused because this enables her to become accustomed to the anxiety in graduated steps and thereby overcome the fear associated with the anxiety. The theory is that over time she will be able to enter the feared situation with increasing equanimity.

The effectiveness of exposure for social phobia has been questioned almost from the time that Marks and Gelder (1966) identified social phobia as a phobia distinct from specific phobias and agoraphobia. Butler (1985) claims that exposure is the most effective treatment for specific phobias and agoraphobia, but acknowledges that it has proven less effective with social phobics. As our concern here is not with specific phobias and agoraphobia, we need not consider her claim that exposure *is* the most effective treatment for specific phobics and agoraphobics. A large research literature, however, demonstrates its effectiveness with specific phobias such as snakes, rats, and small animals (Shorkey & Himle 1974; Öst 1978; Wieselberg et al. 1979; Linden 1981) and with agoraphobics (Hayes & Barlow 1977; Ghosh & Marks 1987). The problems that occur when this method is used with social phobics, however, are that:

1. Tasks cannot always be clearly specified in advance, repeated, or graduated because social situations are variable and unpredictable.

2. Many social situations have an intrinsic time limit and cannot be prolonged. Entering a room, saying good morning, or buying a drink are examples of such situations. Thus, the situation may end before anxiety is aroused.

3. Social phobics often appear to avoid relatively few situations. They may continue to go to work or to other places where they will meet people and may be forced to do some things that provoke

anxiety. This continued exposure, however, is apparently not beneficial because the problem frequently persists despite natural exposure.

4. Thoughts and attitudes seem to play a central role in the maintenance of social phobias. Social phobics are generally preoccupied with the impression they make on others and suppose this to be negative. Exposure, however, provides no information about evaluation and therefore ignores an important aspect of the problem. In contrast, thoughts that accompany agoraphobia—fear of fainting, going crazy, or losing control—appear to subside during exposure. This is probably because exposure provides information that these disasters do not occur and therefore tends to correct the ideas. Such is not the case with thoughts accompanying social phobia. If agoraphobics have their false expectations disconfirmed in the course of exposure, social phobics rarely experience the same obvious disconfirmation.

On the other hand, Butler and her colleagues have found ways to modify the exposure experience for social phobics. They report that these changes have resulted in significant improvements in the social phobics they have treated, even when exposure was the only method used. Instead of specifying tasks in advance and exposing the client to these in a repeated and graduated way, they identify a common theme that is relevant to the individual (essentially what Holt et al. [1992] call "situational domains"). Exposing the client to various situations that meet this common theme is helpful because the different settings shift the focus of practice away from overt social aspects of the difficult situations toward covert cognitive aspects associated with the central fear of negative evaluation. In this way, Butler and associates have been able to achieve a graduated exposure even though the situations and amount of time spent in them are not graduated in the traditional sense. Instead, they instruct clients to begin with situations that they themselves consider easier and to progress to ones they consider harder.

To address the problem that social situations have an intrinsic time limit and cannot be prolonged, clients are encouraged to initiate brief exposures that they are able to repeat at will, such as entering crowded rooms or making inquiries. Many clients have found these brief encounters helpful. Thus, whereas prolonged exposure is needed to disconfirm the agoraphobic's expectation of panicking, even brief social tasks are sufficient to disconfirm the expectations that social phobics have (e.g., being ignored by a desk clerk or salesperson).

Concerning the problem that continued exposure does not lessen the social phobia, Butler notes that at the beginning of treatment roughly 75 percent of her clients reported that they regularly entered the situations that predictably provoked their symptoms but with no lessening of the symptoms. However, when asked to describe these exposures, many clients became aware that they were not fully engaged in these anxiety-arousing activities. They spontaneously reported using a kind of "internal avoidance." For example, one client said that he had learned to "pretend" that he was not in the situation. These self-formulated techniques did not work because they involved dissociating from external rather than internal cues. The problem was how to get clients fully engaged. Butler and her colleagues tried three methods: (1) social skills acquisition, such as listening and speaking skills; (2) the instruction to be active in the situation rather than a passive participant; and (3) the instruction to provoke symptoms of anxiety. Since these procedures were derived from other treatment methods (to be discussed later), Butler's use of them supports the view of most clinicians that exposure alone is insufficient.

Concerning the problem that exposure provides no information about how one is being evaluated by others, Butler reports that phobics who were treated with anxiety management as well as exposure experienced a decrease in perceived negative evaluation while those treated with exposure alone did not. This indicates that the perception of negative evaluation by others is directly linked to the social phobic's belief that she is being negatively evaluated because of her evident anxiety (tremulous voice, shaking hands, etc.). Thus, clients for whom the primary cognitive aspect of the anxiety was that "others will judge my anxiety negatively" were helped by exposure when this exposure included increased skill in anxiety management.

Butler concludes that when social phobics are treated with a relatively pure form of exposure, many complex and interrelated factors may contribute to the effectiveness (or noneffectiveness) of the exposure. For the most part, these other factors have not been made explicit by the exposure method. Thus, the exposure method in its original formulation was based on a simplistic explanation for why exposure may be effective, that is, that gradual exposure to anxiety-arousing stimuli leads to the eventual extinction of the anxiety. Butler argues in favor of the exposure method but she takes seriously the fact that cognitive factors directly influence anxiety levels in social situations. She advocates an exposure treatment with "an active, behavioral, self-help orientation." This self-help orientation is fostered by the development of new social skills and cognitive training in interpreting the behavior of others. These help the social phobic to recognize that the behavior of others is not necessarily evidence of their negative evaluation of the client. This approach is based on the view that reduction of anxiety depends on the full and active engagement of the patient in the exposure, but it draws heavily on other treatment methods to ensure that active engagement does in fact take place (by addressing the "internal avoidance" problem) and that prospects for anxiety reduction are vastly improved (by teaching the client useful social skills).

Perhaps the most important insight that the nonclinician can derive from these modifications of the exposure method is that they challenge the common wisdom that the social phobic will become more comfortable the more she does what she has dreaded doing. Close relatives and friends of social phobics often encourage them to "just do it" in the expectation that the anxiety will gradually decrease and eventually disappear entirely. While this method may be effective with specific phobias, it hasn't worked well with social phobias. The analogy with learning to swim by being thrown into the water is not a good analogy as far as social phobia is concerned. It is much too simplistic.

The Social Skills Treatment Method

Many early efforts to treat social phobics were based on the presumption that clients' anxiety is related to deficient social skills, both verbal (appropriate speech content) and nonverbal (e.g., eye contact, posture, and gestures). Social skills training was believed to increase these behavioral skills, thus removing the underlying cause of anxiety and increasing the probability of successful social outcomes (Heimberg and Juster 1995). Thus, the main assumption of social skills training for social phobia is that "anxiety reduction is the main mechanism of change" and that "skills acquisition is essential for patients with skills deficits" (Wlazlo et al. 1990, 182). This assumption makes a strong association between an individual's anxiety in social situations and her lack of needed social skills to participate in social situations in a nonanxious manner. It is based, in part, on clinically derived evidence that social phobics tend to have less education and to be from lower socioeconomic backgrounds than nonsocial phobics. This evidence has been supported by more recent community-based studies (Schneier et al. 1992), which indicate that the highest rates of social phobia are found among the lowest socioeconomic groups and the most poorly educated. There is also conflicting evidence, however, suggesting that there is no relationship between social phobia and lower educational levels (Rapee

1995). Also, regarding socioeconomic status, Chapman et al. (1995) note that the causal relationship between social phobia and socioeconomic status is complex. While many social phobics may have come from lower socioeconomic backgrounds originally, many others may find themselves relegated to lower socioeconomic status due to their social phobias, which result in their selection into lower status jobs (32).

Another basis for the view that poor social skills are responsible for anxiety in social situations is that social phobia tends to emerge in adolescence. Since teenage social phobics often experience high levels of anxiety in situations requiring formal conversational skills, their anxiety is commonly attributed to social skills deficits. Social skills training (SST) employs modeling, behavioral rehearsal, corrective feedback, social reinforcement, and homework assignments to teach effective social behavior (Heimberg & Juster 1995, 262). These are the types of training techniques that should have appeal and effectiveness with adolescents.

In recent years, however, social skills training for social phobics has been undergoing considerable reevaluation. As Leary and Kowalski (1995) point out, while the social skills deficit theory identified important specific causes of social anxiety, it did not adequately address the question of why poor social skills should make a person nervous in social encounters. Nor did it take account of the fact that many social phobics know what would constitute good social behavior in a given social situation, but their anxiety inhibits them from displaying these skills (94). Thus, while it may be true that they "lack" social skills, this is not because they are unaware of what makes for a good, positive social impression on others. Their problem is that they cannot act on this awareness as a result of their anxiety. Also, as Butler and Wells (1995) note, social skills training typically involves exposure to feared situations and cognitive reappraisal as anxiety decreases and social performance improves. Thus, successful treatment does not necessarily demonstrate that patients need to learn new skills. In fact, the *indirect* effects of social skills training may be responsible for its success. Social skills training may free a person up so that he is able to respond more flexibly to the changing demands of social interactions. Breaking down social performance into its separate skills (observational, listening, nonverbal skills, and so forth) may be helpful when devising practice tasks or helping a client find a way out of a social difficulty. It may also be a useful way of redirecting attention away from internal, distressing anxiety and stimulating cognitive reappraisal. But socially appropriate behavior does not have to be learned in the piecemeal fashion assumed in the earlier application of social skills training. Nor is socially appropriate behavior a guarantee of social success or social comfort (316).

As a result of these criticisms of the social skills training model, current practitioners place greater emphasis on the role that anxiety plays in interfering with the use of social skills. They have developed less "piecemeal" approaches to social skills training. In recognizing that anxiety may be the primary reason that clients are unable to employ the social skills they actually possess, many social skills theorists now believe that the inhibition of social skills in given social situations may be due to other skill deficits, which are themselves due to false or erroneous cognitive beliefs about social relationships and social behavior.

In a recent formulation of the social skills approach to the treatment of shy, socially anxious, and lonely adults, Gambrill (1995) notes that anxiety may interfere with the use of social skills. The social skills that a person already possesses are not used because she lacks self-management skills, or skills in arranging practice opportunities, or because of interfering beliefs about social relationships and social behavior. These incorrect beliefs may in turn interfere with acquisition and use of effective self-management and exposure skills. This implies a complex relationship between anxiety, social skills, other relevant skills, and cognitive beliefs. Gambrill also notes that, where earlier social skills training used a "component model of social behavior" (nods, looks, greetings, and so forth), a "process model of social behavior" has more recently been introduced. It focuses on (1) accurate perception and translation of social cues; (2) the ability to take the role of others; (3) nonverbal communication of attitudes and emotions; (4) offering others clear reinforcement and rewards; (5) planning goals and altering behavior as required; (6) sending social signals that accurately present one's roles, status, and other elements of social identity; (7) skill in analyzing situations and their rules to adapt behavior effectively; and (8) verbal behavior that fits into the orderly sequence of social exchanges. Thus, social *skill* now refers to the process of generating skilled behavior directed toward a goal, social *competence* refers to the capacity to generate skilled behavior, and social *performance* refers to the production of skilled behavior in specific situations. While discrete social skills are still important, they are now considered integral to the larger social process.

A key feature of this shift in emphasis from discrete behaviors to larger components of social competence is that "goal setting" assumes much greater importance. A person enters the social situation with certain preplanned goals and seeks to achieve these goals or creatively alter them to other goals in the course of the social interaction. Gambrill notes that clients usually focus on defensive goals such as avoiding making a poor impression rather than trying to create a favorable one.

A process-oriented social skills approach encourages an emphasis on favorable outcomes, not just the avoidance of unfavorable ones. She points out that the importance of considering positive as well as negative goals is supported by research that indicates the relative independence of negative and positive affect. Also, intermediate goals such as having a brief, pleasant conversation are often dismissed by clients as irrelevant to their ultimate objective of making close friends or finding a romantic partner. Thus, clients are encouraged to view intermediate steps as being valuable in their own right.

On the other hand, while social skills practitioners are taking the whole social process itself more seriously, they have not abandoned their earlier emphasis on teaching specific social skills. As Donahue et al. (1994) point out, a common technique of social skills therapists is role-playing. Role-played social scenarios are directly observed or videotaped. They are then retrospectively rated on a variety of verbal and nonverbal components identified in prior social skills research as requisite to interpersonal effectiveness. Verbal components include speech duration, voice tone, and the like, while nonverbal components include expressive gestures, eye contact, smiles, and similar gestures. Examples of role-play themes with social phobics include meeting new friends, giving speeches in front of a group, and maintaining conversations with others. In her discussion of the kinds of skills that therapists continue to stress in the treatment of social phobics, Gambrill points out that valuable opportunities to meet others are often lost because of reticence or lack of skill in initiating conversation. Or a client may have appropriate skills for initiating conversation but may display these at the wrong time. Even though clients may know a variety of ways to initiate conversation, they may benefit from learning and practicing additional one. Nonverbal behaviors that are important in initiating conversations include eye contact, pleasant facial expression, and body orientation toward the other person. Voice qualities such as loudness and a relative absence of hesitations and stammers may influence success. Vocal training may be needed to enhance delivery. Other skills included in training programs are giving and receiving compliments, refusing unwanted requests, requesting changes in annoying behaviors, handling silences, altering participation in conversation (talking more or less), and sharing feelings.

Gambrill emphasizes, however, that the discrete social skills introduced by the therapist need to be directly relevant to the client's achievement of clearly identified and articulated goals. If a client wishes to become a more skilled conversationalist, the therapist may employ role-play to discover the client's conversational weaknesses. For example, a client may use only one way to initiate a conversation and may benefit from broadening her repertoire. Another client may have found that he has the social skills needed for the beginning stages of relationships but does not know how to move the relationship to a deeper level. The therapist may inform the client that increased self-disclosure is necessary to move a relationship to a deeper level and help him practice engaging in such self-disclosure. Gambrill is critical of most training programs designed to help shy and socially inhibited persons because they often fail to include assessment of each client's social skills relevant to desired outcomes and pay little or no attention to identification of social skills needed to enhance success in real-life settings.

A complicating factor in social skills assessment and acquisition is the matter of self-management skills. By self-management skills, Gambrill means the ability to monitor one's actions and behaviors, to assess the impact of other persons' actions on one's own actions, and to make the kinds of judgments and decisions that maximize the opportunities afforded by social interactive situations. Many shy, lonely, or socially anxious persons have correct knowledge about social skills and when to use them, but they do not do so. They fail to arrange for opportunities to use their skills or to overcome or diminish social anxiety by exposure to feared situations. Persons with poor self-management skills do not know how to (1) select specific long-term and short-term goals or intermediate steps; (2) select clear, achievable, and relevant assignments; (3) motivate themselves; (4) monitor their progress; and (5) take successful corrective steps based on the degree of progress already made. Thus, the absence of a skill-based conceptualization of social comfort and success makes it unlikely that self-management skills would be viewed as relevant to attaining social goals.

Self-management skills are also necessary to gain access to promising social contexts, for even with excellent social skills, clients who do not seek out opportunities to use their skill will not achieve valued social goals. For example, one study showed that if a man liked a woman but was not actually thinking about dating women, there was only a 2 percent likelihood that he would ask this woman out on a date. Not thinking of dating is a self-management issue. It may also be related to a cognitive issue such as the assumption that his liking for this woman could not possibly be reciprocated or the belief that if he pursues this relationship he will only experience hurt again. In this way, a negative cognitive process may contribute to inadequate self-management skills.

Gambrill concludes that the effectiveness of social skills training depends in part on the therapist's success in providing a rationale for social skills training, as most clients "do not think of the quality of their social life as being partly skill-based. Rather, they usually have a variety of misconceptions about social behavior, most of which either offer no guidelines for positive change or provide misleading directions" (268–269). A basic assumption of the social skills approach is that "anxiety in social situations is…a learned reaction resulting from previous social experiences, which can be unlearned by corrective learning experiences" (269).

Heimberg and Juster (1995) point out that the social skills approach makes considerable use of exposure because it assumes that the social skills acquired through instruction, rehearsal, and role-playing need to be tested in real-life situations. This approach also assumes, however, that merely exposing an individual to anxiety-arousing situations is insufficient because his anxiety will not decrease merely because he is able to remain in the situation for increasing periods of time. Butler and Wells (1995) believe that the ability to remain in a situation is not necessarily due to the fact that a person is using newly acquired social skills. Rather, it has more to do with the indirect effects of social skills training, which seems to free a person up so that she is able to respond more flexibly to the changing demands of social interactions. This point is supported by Wlazlo and his colleagues (1990) who, by using a combined exposure and social skills approach, found that it is much more effective to teach patients a single and generally applicable social strategy than to teach specific coping strategies for different social situations. They emphasize training in social competence, but they think of this in terms of increased social perception and discrimination and less in terms of the more traditional approach of instructing patients in such skills as learning how to make requests, refuse the requests of others, and so on. They have also found that this learning was best achieved through a process of group exposure: "Compared to individual exposure, the group exposure has the advantage that group cohesion and modeling can enhance the effectiveness of the exposure technique. Further, especially in the exposure mode a general coping strategy for social situations is taught" (191).

In short, Wlazlo and his associates believe that the learning of a good "coping strategy" through direct involvement in a group exposure process is more effective than learning specific social skills designed to overcome a particular person's assessed deficits. On the other hand, one of the improvements that the clients in the Wlazlo et al. study identified as important to them personally was their improvement in social skills. Whatever the actual reason for their improvement may have been, they personally believed that it was due to the fact that they had acquired better social skills.

Perhaps the most important insight the nonclinician can derive from the social skills approach to treatment of social phobics is the fact that most social phobics are fully aware of what makes for good social communication and interaction. They simply find themselves unable—as a result of anxiety—to act on this knowledge. Their awareness is reflected in their ability to make accurate judgments about other persons' social performances, an ability developed through years of adopting a submissive, and thus observational position in social gatherings. This observational skill, however, may become a serious handicap, as it increases the social phobic's awareness of all the many ways in which one can perform badly in social situations, thus increasing his self-consciousness when he tries to perform well. Social skills training can be helpful in overcoming such self-consciousness, but the social phobic may be prone to set a very high standard for herself as far as social skills ability is concerned, and she may therefore be highly aware of how far short she falls of genuine social effectiveness. Thus, social skills training may play into the social phobic's perfectionism.

The Behavioral Treatment Method

A major premise of behavioral treatment for social phobia is that social phobias are learned behavior and that they are learned in one of two ways. The first is that they are learned through "autonomic conditioning," meaning that a person has experienced anxiety in one or more social situations and is therefore conditioned to fear such situations. The goal of therapy is to help the client "unlearn" what he has learned, which may be accomplished by various methods, especially systematic desensitization and controlled exposure, so that the previous association between anxiety and the social situation no longer obtains. The other way that social phobia is learned is by the modeling or instructional/informational behavior of another person or persons (Öst 1985). A child may observe her parent becoming anxious in a given social situation and develop the same anxiety. Or a child is warned by her parent that a particular social situation is dangerous, and develops an anxious response to this situation. What these learning processes share in common is that the learning is indirect.

While we might assume that direct experience of the phobic situation is a more powerful "conditioner" than either modeling or instruction/information, this is not necessarily the case. After all, many children and adults experience severe anxieties about objects or situations they have never directly experienced (such as ghosts, hell, etc.). Also, the methods used to help clients "unlearn" phobias acquired through indirect means are essentially the same as those for phobias acquired through direct involvement. However, in a study by Öst (1985) it was found that a significantly larger proportion of phobics acquired their phobias through direct rather than indirect conditioning experiences. Among the social phobics, 56 percent acquired their phobia through direct conditioning, 16 percent through modeling, 3 percent through instructional/ informational behavior, and 25 percent had no recall of the circumstances that caused the phobia to develop.

The behavioral treatment of social phobics emphasizes accurate clinical assessment. Behavioral therapists employ a structured clinical interview leading to an evaluation and treatment plan. The interview focuses on self-report and reports by others. These include family members and friends and usually also include members of the therapeutic team who have observed the client enter the clinic, ask for directions, and so on. As Donahue et al. (1994) point out, behavioral assessment of social phobia may include a variety of self-report strategies, including behavioral interviews, structured inventories, self-monitoring, and protocol analysis. The behavioral interview is used to obtain a detailed analysis of the client's interpersonal history and description of current level of functioning. Frequencies and magnitude of problems experienced in social situations are thoroughly reviewed. These may include interactions with persons of the same gender versus the other gender, public speaking, casual and more intimate relationships, number of persons in the interactions, and initiating and maintaining relationships, and more. Following this review, the client's level of social skill is ascertained for possible modification.

As the treatment process continues, various inventories are used to monitor progress, most of which are also based on self-report. At present, there are three self-report inventories for assessment of social phobia. The Social Interaction Self-Statement Test (SISST), for example, consists of fifteen positive and fifteen negative thoughts associated with anxiety-evoking situations (e.g., "I am really afraid of what they'll think of me"). Each thought is rated on a five-point scale according to the frequency with which it occurs in socially problematic situations. Self-monitoring strategies are also employed. In these procedures, clients typically record targeted behaviors that occur in anxiety-eliciting social situations. Information obtained from self-monitoring can be used to assess stimuli that are anxiety provoking, the efficacy of intervention procedures, and the maintenance and generalizability of acquired skills.

Protocol analysis involves organizing clients' self-statements into content or themes. Thus, the thought "I am going to say something stupid" is placed under the content domain of "fear of making foolish comments while speaking." Clients are asked to record the frequency of such thoughts during anxiety-arousing situations. Progress is then assessed by comparing these frequencies at various phases of the treatment.

To assess overt behavior in social situations, behavioral therapists use role-playing. Role-played social scenarios are directly observed or videotaped and then rated on a variety of verbal and nonverbal components similar to those used in social skills training (e.g., speech duration, voice tone, expressive gestures, eye contact, smiles). Examples of role-play themes with social phobics include meeting new friends, giving speeches in front of a group, and carrying on conversations with others. Role-play is often used concurrently with physiological assessment devices. For example, heart rate response has proven to be a fairly reliable discriminator between social phobics and control subjects and between subtypes of social phobics (McNeil et al. 1995). Blushing is another physiological reaction that can be measured by using a photoplethysomograph. The two major bases for assessment of role-play interactions are social skills and anxiety. The client is asked to rate her performances on these two scales, and then trained, independent judges rate her videotaped performances later. These two ratings have been the basis for the commonly-noted fact that social phobics tend to rate themselves more negatively than independent judges do.

Efforts to develop better behavioral methods for evaluating role-played performances are continually being made. Some of these tests and inventories are quite complex. For example, the Social Interaction Test (SIT) includes twenty-nine ratings of verbal, nonverbal, and other categories of social behavior. These ratings are performed by judges and by the other person or persons in the role-play. Rating devices have also been developed to determine a client's social skills. There are two types of behavioral assessment tests (BATS), standardized and individually tailored. The three primary types of standardized tests are conversation with a same-gender stranger, with an other-gender stranger, and an impromptu speech to a small audience. The individually tailored tests include interacting in a group conversation or starting a conversation with a person one may want to ask out on a date. Important variations are the degree to which role-played situations involve instructional control of interactions, such as whether the participants are provided with choices of speech topics or not (McNeill et al. 1995).

Another important variation is the measurement of avoidance (not entering the situation at all) and escape (entering the situation but leaving it prematurely). Earlier tests did not permit avoidance and escape but more recent ones have incorporated this variation into the test design. Some tests have provided a motoric response (e.g., raising a "stop sign") to allow clients to terminate a step in the test. Non-overt behaviors of avoidance and escape are also assessed, such as "freezing" during delivery of a speech, camouflage (e.g., hiding by being a "wallflower" in a social gathering), and submission (e.g., social appeasement).

As this summary of the behavioral approach indicates, considerable emphasis is placed on assessment both before and during the treatment period. Follow-up assessments are also conducted. While behavioral therapists depend on assessment in order to achieve therapeutic gains, they also make direct interventions in the treatment process, including social skills training, relaxation training, and guided exposure involving real-life as opposed to role-play situations. Over the past several years, they have focused increasingly on the cognitive dimension of social phobia, especially the influence of negative thoughts in increasing and maintaining anxiety, in precipitating avoidance and escape behaviors, and so forth. Cognitive restructuring is now a regular feature of behavioral therapy for social phobics (Donahue et al. 1994).

The effectiveness of behavioral therapy largely depends on the effectiveness of the specific interventions employed. Because various methods are commonly used (social skills training, relaxation training, guided exposure, and cognitive restructuring), determining which method or methods accounted for a client's improvement is often impossible. Given their behavioral orientation, behavioral therapists have been among the most research oriented of the social phobic clinicians. Many research studies, however, have produced inconclusive or contradictory evidence regarding the relative effectiveness of the various therapeutic methods employed. The picture is complicated by the fact that there are different types of social phobia, and research studies will often claim that a given method proved more effective with one type than the others. On the other hand, behavioral therapists are generally moving to the view that therapeutic results are improved when they include a "cognitive restructuring" component. As we have seen, Heimberg and Barlow (1988; also Heimberg and Juster, 1995) refer to "cognitive-behavioral" therapy, indicating that clinicians are increasingly reluctant to use "behavioral" methods alone.

Perhaps the most important insight of the behavioral treatment method for the nonclinician is that the social phobic is helped by diverting or shifting his attention from his inner state of anxiety to his external behavior. By dissociating himself from inner processes and focusing on external ones, his anxiety may decrease simply because he is no longer so aware of it. The assumption that social phobia is learned and can therefore (at least in principle) be unlearned is, however, open to serious question. As we saw in our earlier discussion of behaviorally inhibited children, there are undoubtedly biological or genetic factors operative as well. The power of such factors should not be minimized. To do so can create false hope and expectations on the part of family members and friends and the social phobic himself. This can be especially damaging if the social phobic's failure to make substantial process is subject to moral judgments, whether one's own or those of relatives and friends.

The Self-efficacy Treatment Method

Another early-established method is the "self-efficacy" approach. This approach is based on the theory developed by Bandura (Bandura et al. 1980) that a person's perceived efficacy enhances psychosocial functioning. When applied to phobics, this theory does not focus on the anxiety-eliciting features of feared social situations and thus the goal of reducing anxiety. Instead, it centers on a person's perception of his ability to cope with specific threats. It emphasizes what the person believes she can do, and defines progress in terms of coping capacity or self-efficacy ("I can do this"). In their description of the self-efficacy method, Williams et al. (1985) note that performance success rather than the passage of time is the critical therapeutic ingredient. Because prescribing success does not ensure that a client will actually achieve it, the therapist takes a highly active role in giving the client direct assistance and behavioral guidance during her performance efforts. Such aid is designed to enhance her ability to initiate new activities and to execute tasks in ways that create a robust sense of personal capability.

The self-efficacy treatment model was initially developed for specific phobics and agoraphobics (Williams et al. 1985; Williams and Kleifield 1985). Clients with a fear of heights were taken to an eight-story parking garage and asked to indicate, on a scale of ten to one hundred, whether they believed they could ascend to each floor of the building and how confident they felt about being able to do so. Self-efficacy strength was the sum of the confidence ratings divided by the number of floors. Thus a rating of ten indicated that a client felt that ascending to any floor was a virtual impossibility. The guided mastery feature of the treatment involved informing clients to tackle more difficult tasks as rapidly as possible. When they experienced difficulty in making progress, the therapist would provide a variety of performance induction aids and behavioral guidance. For example, clients sometimes had problems with specific aspects of a task, such as being able to do everything but look down when standing by the railing. They were encouraged to practice looking at the ground when far from the railing, then continue to look down as they progressed toward it. To help ensure that successful performance would impart a feeling of genuine accomplishment, clients were guided to perform tasks in a variety of ways, such as standing with their backs to the railing.

Summarizing these guided mastery features, Williams et al. indicate that guided mastery treatment includes two major components: (1) when clients are having difficulty progressing, the therapist uses performance aids to help restore effective coping; and (2) after functioning has been reinstated, the therapist withdraws the provisional aids and arranges for varied and independent success experiences to authenticate and generalize clients' sense of mastery. The choice of aids is determined by their potential impact on perceived self-efficacy. When the given task is too formidable, therapists suggest proximal performance goals because people often believe themselves capable of tackling more manageable proximate goals. Also, because awkwardness and self-protective activities undermine self-efficacy by making clients feel inept, mastery-oriented therapists guide clients in performing tasks in proficient and varied ways.

Proponents of this method argue that its success is due to the fact that "people are asked to do as much as they can do, and this is in fact what they feel motivated to do" (Williams 1992, 155). In their view, a client's view of what she can accomplish is the most important determinant of what she is, in fact, able to accomplish. While self-efficacy treatment involves exposure, exposure as such does not account for improvement. The modeling and guidance provided by a mastery-oriented therapist enhances the client's sense of self-efficacy, and this is what makes self-efficacy more successful than merely exposing her to anxiety-arousing situations (Williams 1987, 1988).

As noted, self-efficacy treatment has tended to focus on specific phobias and agoraphobia. However, a self-efficacy questionnaire for social skills (SEQSS) has been developed (see Elting and Hope 1995, 235) in which subjects are presented with twelve social situations and asked to rate their expected social behavior in these situations. This questionnaire has not been extensively used in clinical practice, so it remains unclear whether clients' perceived self-efficacy in *social* situations typically experienced as distressing to social phobics makes a significant difference. One obvious problem that social phobia presents for this treatment method is the difficulty of incorporating guided mastery into exposure to a social situation, since the mere presence of the therapist will dramatically alter the situation itself. Also, the situation may significantly influence the degree to which the therapist is able to provide guidance and support. While the therapist might model good conversational skills in an informal social situation at which the client is also present, the client will not necessarily have opportunity to practice these skills immediately after the therapist demonstrates them. Even if the opportunity does present itself, the client may be concerned that the other persons present will perceive him to be imitating or even mimicking the therapist. These and various other dilemmas that the reader can readily imagine appear to make the self-efficacy model less accessible to social phobia than to the other phobias.

Its basic theoretical point—that belief in one's ability to cope with a given situation has a profound effect on how he actually behaves in that situation—is, however, a very important one. A therapist does well to ascertain a client's self-efficacy beliefs before instructing or encouraging her to enter a feared social situation. Exposing a client to a situation without first ascertaining her degree of confidence that she will be able to cope with the experience may lead to failure and thus cause the phobia to become even more resistant to change. As Williams (1987) points out: "The exposure principle not only fails to advance understanding of mechanisms, but it gives therapists little guidance in how to implement treatments most effectively. Progress in developing better treatments is clearly necessary, as a distressingly large percentage of phobics fail to benefit much from current treatments based on stimulus exposure and anxiety extinction" (173).

Perhaps the most important insight of the self-efficacy treatment model for non-clinicians is that it credits the social phobic with knowing what is possible for her and what is impossible. Trusting the social phobic to make her own judgments and determinations takes seriously the fact that social phobia is an anxiety disorder and that a major feature of social phobia is anticipatory anxiety or dread. To expect or require the social phobic to undergo an experience that evokes excessive anticipatory anxiety is unlikely to be helpful in the long run. My experience of social phobics is that they do not totally avoid social situations that they truly need—and want—to attend, such as the marriage of their son or daughter or the funeral of an immediate member of the family. (Their difficulty is in giving a toast or eulogy on these occasions).

This, it seems to me, should be taken into account when the social phobic finds it too unnerving to attend a social gathering that is less obligatory or chooses not to perform at a meeting where other qualified speakers are available and are quite happy to do so. This does not, of course, mean that the social phobic should not attempt to stretch herself or should use her phobia as merely a convenient excuse to avoid an unpleasant social gathering or meeting. As we have seen, however, the social phobic is affiliative by nature and therefore tends to make decisions *not* to attend and *not* to perform for reasons other than laziness or unwillingness to prepare.

Conclusion

I have considered several treatment methods that were developed and refined during the first two decades following the official identification of social phobia in 1966. Two of these methods, exposure and behavioral therapy, reflect the belief that social phobia has significant similarities to the other types of phobias. In these two approaches, treatments for social phobia are fundamentally no different from methods employed with specific phobics and agoraphobics. They give primary emphasis to exposure to the feared situation and, through relaxation and desensitization techniques, seek to eliminate the physiological arousal (or anxiety) involved. The treatment method that was explicitly designed for social phobia is social skills training. This method is of little value for specific phobias and usually unnecessary for agoraphobia. Its effectiveness for social phobia has also been questioned, but as these questions have arisen, the method has been modified to address them. The self-efficacy model is an especially interesting case. While its primary use has been with specific phobias and agoraphobia, its central assumption (that the client's own beliefs about himself and his coping abilities are the crucial element in the treatment plan and its ultimate outcome) anticipates the cognitive-behavioral treatment method to be discussed in the next chapter. This is because it focuses on the client's own cognitions, his assumptions and beliefs about the feared situation, and his own ability to cope with it. Thus, while not as extensively used with social phobics as exposure and behavioral therapies, the self-efficacy treatment method may be viewed as a bridge to the treatment method we will consider in the next chapter.

CHAPTER 5

Cognitive-Behavioral Therapy

In this chapter, I will focus on the cognitive-behavioral treatment approach to social phobia. Widely employed in the treatment of many other disorders, cognitive-behavioral therapy has been used in social phobia treatment for somewhat more than a decade, long enough for researchers and clinicians to assess its effectiveness. This method has roots in the behavioral approach. However, unlike the original behavioral model, which views anxiety as a physiological response only, the cognitive-behavioral method recognizes that social phobias also involve cognitions, that is, assumptions and beliefs about social situations and one's own ability to cope with them. As we have seen, the self-efficacy model also emphasizes the client's beliefs about her ability to cope with certain feared situations, but the full recognition of the importance of both negative and positive cognitions for social phobia reflects the influence of the work of Beck and his associates on a variety of psychological disorders (Beck et al. 1985).

An example of the cognitive-behavioral approach to social phobia is a model developed by Clark and Wells (1995). This model recognizes the individual's strong desire to convey a particular favorable impression of himself to others and marked insecurity about his ability to do so. Due to previous experiences interacting with innate behavioral dispositions, social phobics develop a series of assumptions about themselves and their social world that make them prone to believe that they are in danger in one or more social situations. Specifically, they believe that when they enter such situations, they are in danger of behaving in an inept and unacceptable fashion, and that such behavior will have disastrous consequences in terms of loss of status, loss of worth, and rejection. Once the social phobic perceives a social situation in this way, an "anxiety program" is automatically and reflexively activated.

Clark and Wells recognize that this anxiety program is a complex constellation of cognitive, somatic, affective, and behavioral changes inherited from our evolutionary past and originally designed to protect us from harm in objectively dangerous primitive environments. When the danger is more imagined than real, however, these anxiety responses are largely inappropriate. Instead of serving a useful function, they often become further sources of perceived danger. In this way, they contribute to a series of vicious cycles that tend to maintain or exacerbate social anxiety. Social phobics also become preoccupied with their somatic responses and negative social-evaluative thoughts, and this preoccupation interferes with their ability to process social cues, an effect that they notice and take as further evidence of social threat and failure.

Clark and Wells' cognitive model assumes that social phobics' interpretation of social situations as threatening is the consequence of a series of dysfunctional beliefs that they hold about themselves and about the way they should behave in social situations. The model identifies three categories of dysfunctional beliefs: excessively high standards for social performance; conditional beliefs about social evaluation; and unconditional beliefs about the self.

Examples of excessively high standards for social performance are "I must get everyone's approval," "I must not show any signs of weakness," "I must not let anyone see that I am anxious," and "I must appear intelligent and witty." High standards generate anxiety because they are very difficult to achieve. As a result, social phobics are constantly concerned that they may fail to convey the desired favorable impression.

Examples of conditional beliefs about social evaluation are "If I show feelings or make mistakes others will reject me," "If others really get to know me, they won't like me," and "If I disagree with someone, they will think I'm stupid."

Typical unconditional beliefs about the self are "I'm odd or peculiar," "I'm different," "I'm unacceptable," "I'm stupid," "I'm unattractive," "I'm vulnerable," and "I'm inadequate." These unconditional beliefs about the self are the basic "self-schemata" of a social phobic. In contrast to depressives, who have a similar self-schemata, social phobics' self-schemata are unstable. That is, in social situations they have a more negative, uncertain view of themselves, whereas when alone or in nonthreatening social situations they often have a more positive view of themselves. The feeling that they are different, odd, and inadequate is mainly triggered, and seems compelling, when they are with people who are thought to be evaluating them.

With most social phobics, the unconditional beliefs about the self develop first, perhaps as a result of having been shy or behaviorally-inhibited as a child. Excessively high standards and conditional beliefs about social evaluation emerge later as a part of a compensating or protective strategy. In these cases, the self-schemata feels "ego-syntonic" ("It's me"). However, there are other cases of social phobia in which an individual develops conditional beliefs about social evaluation, perhaps as a result of having performed badly in public gatherings. The resulting negative self-schemata is then experienced as ego-dystonic ("It's not me"). For example, a young newspaper editor who had an exceptional career and was awarded a prize as the nation's most promising newcomer drank too much alcohol before his acceptance speech. As he began speaking, he noticed he had difficulty finding some words and that he was sweating. He became convinced that other people noticed these failings and he rapidly developed a public speaking phobia. For him, the self-schemata that developed from this experience was ego-dystonic.

Safety-behaviors are another aspect of the Clark and Wells model. These are the techniques, devices, and strategies that social phobics develop as a means to reduce the risk of negative evaluation. The problem with such behaviors is that they prevent the social phobic from experiencing an unambiguous disconfirmation of her unrealistic beliefs. In some instances they can make the feared behaviors more likely to occur. For example, a woman who grasped her wine glass very tightly discovered that this made her hand more likely to shake.

In an extensive table, Clark and Wells present a variety of cases from their own clinical practice. A much shortened version of this table (five cases) appears in table 3. The first three cases are women, the fourth and fifth are men. The model is represented by the categories indicated at the top of the table: feared situation, negative self-evaluation, negative thoughts about others, information used to infer others' reactions, safety behaviors, and self-schemata assumptions.

The first case involves a clergywoman who fears administering the chalice during the communion service. Her negative self-evaluation in the situation is based on the apprehension that she will spill the wine and thus confirm her belief that she "always" gets things wrong and "always" messes up. Her negative thoughts about others are that they will criticize her and question her ability to perform this task. The information she uses to support this view of their anticipated reaction is her own self-image as one who loses control in trying situations and the negative feelings that some parishioners have about women priests.

Table 3: Cognitive-Behavioral Model of Social Phobia Class

Feared Situation(s)	Negative Self-evaluation	Negative Thoughts about Others	Information Used to Infer Others' Reaction	Safety Behaviors	Assumptions and Self-schemata [a]
Administering chalice in church.	I'll lose control and shake. My hands are paralyzed. I'll spill the wine. I always get things wrong. Idiot-woman, why do I always mess up?	They'll see me shake. They'll criticize me. They'll think I can't do it.	Shaking. Image of self losing control. Negative feeling of some parishioners about women priests.	Take beta blockers. Control breathing. Grip chalice tightly. Move hands slowly. Focus on hands. Don't overfill chalice.	I have to get everything right or I'll be rejected (s). If someone dislikes me, I'm a failure (c). If people don't accept me, I'm worthless (c). I'm worthless (u). I'm a failure (u).
Being in formal meetings.	I'll lose control. I'll break down and cry. Panic will take over.	They won't respect me. They won't like me. They'll pity me.	Feeling of wanting to cry. Blushing. Someone joked about blushing. Image of self in anxious situation.	Avoid situation. Say less. Avoid eye contact.	If people think badly of me, then I am bad (c). I'm weak (u).
Reading in group. New social situations.	I'll go red. I'm unable to talk. I'll lose bladder control. I'll look stupid. I'll totally clam up. I'll shake.	They'll reject me. People don't like me.	Imagines how people will react in advance of situation. Focuses on sensations.	Slow breathing. Distraction. Talk/read slowly. Stand still. Try to look confident. Positive self-talk.	I must get everyone's approval (s). If people see me shake, it means I'm inferior to them (c). If people see how I feel, it means I'm different (c). Being different means I'll end up alone, rejected, isolated (c). I'm odd, peculiar (u). I'm different (u).
One-to-one social encounters.	I'll say the wrong thing. I won't be able to talk. I'm paralyzed. I'll freeze. I'll choke. I haven't got anything worthwhile to say.	They'll criticize me. They'll think I'm boring. They don't want to know me.	Visualizes things going wrong. Postmortem.	Do not think about self. Self-monitor thoughts. Talk less.	I have to say something witty, intelligent, and interesting or people won't like me (s). If I'm quiet, people will think I'm boring (c). I'm inadequate (u).
Speaking to a group. Serving drinks.	I'm making a fool of myself. I'm losing control. I can't get the words out.	They'll think I'm stupid. People will stare. They'll think I'm not confident.	Shaking. Subjective difficulty talking. Image of losing self-control.	Distraction. Use mugs. Avoid situation. Say less. Mentally rehearse sentences. Avoid eye contact. Don't talk about self.	I'm vulnerable (u).

[a] s: excessively high standards; c: conditional beliefs; u: unconditional beliefs

Safety behaviors that she has used include pharmacological remedies and various methods for exercising self-control. Her excessively high standards for social performance are reflected in her belief that she must get everything right or she will be rejected. Her conditional beliefs about social evaluation involve the idea that if others dislike her or don't accept her, she is a failure and a worthless person. Her unconditional beliefs about herself are that she is indeed worthless, powerless, and a failure. These unconditional beliefs (self-schemata) are especially germane to social situations in which she is performing as a priest. She may not hold these beliefs in other nonthreatening social situations or when she is alone.

In setting forth their cognitive model of social phobia, Clark and Wells do not address the matter of treatment. Butler and Wells (1995), however, present the clinical applications of the model. Their discussion of the process of cognitive therapy begins by emphasizing the therapist's need to be sensitive to the ways in which social phobia may interfere with the treatment process. The social awkwardness that springs from anxiety about being evaluated will almost certainly occur during therapy itself. When this happens, clients often become increasingly self-aware. Their attention may be distracted by self-denigrative thoughts or by sensations associated with embarrassment. This makes it hard for them to concentrate on what is being said or to remain fully engaged in the process of therapy. Therapists need to watch out for this, because when it occurs it often becomes necessary to repeat key ideas more than once, to make use of frequent summaries, and to encourage clients to give feedback and to write down the points they want to remember.

The process of cognitive therapy itself involves asking many questions intended to help clients look for new perspectives and new ways of seeing things. But sometimes this questioning method can provoke sufficient anxiety to inhibit, rather than facilitate, disclosure. The less the client is able to say, the more questions the therapist asks and the more the therapist does the talking. The vicious cycle that maintains anxiety outside the session may thus exert its influence in the session itself. In this awkward situation, the therapist's most important skill is flexibility so as to find other ways to collect the same information. If the client discloses very little, it helps to use statements and reflections rather than direct questions. For example, "It must have been difficult for you," "I would like to know more about that," "I wonder if...?" "You thought you were making an idiot of yourself," and so forth.

The therapist also needs to be aware that there are many different sources of social discomfort, any one of which may be present in therapy itself. For example, some people find that conventional degrees of interpersonal proximity provoke anxiety and that they respond better if given more physical space. Some need extra time to think about what they want to say, and their anxiety increases if they feel rushed. Others feel more awkward if faced with a silence and become more comfortable if the therapist bridges gaps and keeps the interaction moving. Skilled therapists can adapt their use of gestures and eye contact to set the client at ease. If sensitively used, these aspects of the therapeutic interaction can facilitate the process of therapy, which may otherwise suffer from the same kind of social awkwardness that occurs elsewhere. On the other hand, the therapist should guard against making therapy completely safe, because this will remove vital opportunities for exploring fears and challenging beliefs.

The primary goal of cognitive therapy is to achieve cognitive change. This involves challenging and replacing assumptions and beliefs relating to the three areas of excessively high standards for social performance, conditional beliefs about social evaluation, and unconditional beliefs about the self. Butler and Wells (1995) emphasize the importance of identifying the precise form and idiosyncratic content of each person's cognitions. A cognitive treatment that attends insufficiently to the individualized nature of thoughts and beliefs may lose much of its potential and fail to help clients develop a new way of thinking about social interactions and the risks or threats that they perceive in them. They note that the theory behind cognitive treatments is relatively straightforward, but its applications may be quite difficult, and therapists can fall into many traps along the way. The most common are labeling the clients' thoughts as irrational and necessarily wrong, providing alternative suggestions instead of encouraging clients to come up with and evaluate their own ideas, and merely asking clients to replace one kind of thought with another. Cognitive therapists need to listen to, elucidate, and join in the reexamination of each client's internal dialogue without giving the impression that there is a right and a wrong way of thinking.

Combining the cognitive work with relevant behavioral exposure tasks also seems helpful, but the therapist needs to ensure that the cognitive procedures and exposure experiences are fully integrated. Cognitive therapists operate on different assumptions than "pure" behavioral therapists and social skills therapists. The cognitive approach contends that exposure is effective when it modifies the negative beliefs that underlie the client's problems. Change does not depend on the duration, frequency, or graduated nature of the exposure, but on the opportunity the exposure provides for both activating the customary fear and disconfirming the beliefs associated with it. If the fear is not activated, the client may claim that the experience was irrelevant or only tangentially relevant to the problem. If a genuine exposure does occur, this should be followed by therapeutic measures designed to disconfirm the belief.

Heimberg et al. (1985) illustrate how this post-exposure cognitive restructuring is conducted. The client is first asked to recall his thoughts during the exposure. Reported cognitions fall into a few relatively homogeneous categories, including concern that others would detect her anxiety and evaluate her negatively, fears of embarrassment and humiliation, and negative evaluation of her own social performance. We saw this, for example, in the case of the woman priest. While several techniques are used in the cognitive restructuring component, the primary approach involves repeated and persistent questioning of the client along the lines of, "What does it mean if...?," "What would you have had to do in order to feel good about...?," and "What is the evidence for...?" Repeating the "What does it mean if...?" question is helpful in revealing the client's basic fear. For example, a client's concerns over someone's detecting her nervousness may be found to be based on a fear that she will live out her life in utter isolation. Once revealed, the unsupportable logic of her fear and the actual probability of the consequence is then examined. The question, "What would you have had to do in order to feel good about...?," helps to identify the client's application of unattainable standards to the evaluation of her own behavior and subsequent negative self-evaluations. The question, "What is the evidence for...?" allows for the creation of behavioral experiments to test the validity of the client's beliefs. A belief, typically construed as a fact by the client, is cast as a hypothesis that may then be evaluated.

One of the things that inhibits the effectiveness of an exposure is the safety behaviors that social phobics develop to insulate them from their social anxiety. Like behavioral therapy, cognitive therapy involves instructing the client to enter the feared situation without using safety behaviors. Because this instruction is difficult for the client to implement, cognitive therapists give considerable attention to ways of helping him carry through on it. For example, the therapist might instruct him to make a deliberate mistake in a speech, or deliberately drop something on the floor, or purposely forget someone's name. Since these are actions that the client has worked hard to avoid because of feared negative reaction, the act of committing them enables him to experience and witness the actual consequences of these behaviors. As the consequences usually are not those that he feared, these paradoxical tests provide excellent opportunities for the disconfirmation of his negative beliefs. Mersch et al. (1992) report on a socially phobic woman who was instructed to tremble on social occasions. She was extremely anxious prior to this exercise but during the exercise itself her anxiety decreased and most of the time it completely disappeared. After a few experiences involving deliberate tremblings, her use of alcohol at receptions and parties was dramatically less than before. She also found that she had become more assertive, daring to express her opinions to other persons and to question the opinions of others. Cognitive therapists also employ homework assignments. These focus on encouraging the client to think of alternative ways of interpreting the thoughts of others toward oneself. Table 4 (adapted from Butler and Wells 1995) provides an example of one client's written homework. In each instance, she expresses her usual interpretation of what others are thinking and then considers other possibilities. These other possibilities are both more likely and less judgmental toward her.

TABLE 4
Examples of a Client's Written Homework

The Incident	What I Think People Think	Other Possibilities
Took brother to airport and cried in public.	Strangers can see me for what I am, which is weak.	It's a natural reaction in an airport.
Reaching up to fill machine with coffee beans.	She looks nervous. She's got wet armpits.	Maybe they just observe me without judging me.
Bus driver catches my eye.	He thinks that I'm a weirdo and regrets saying good morning to me.	Maybe he is indifferent. He says the same to everyone.
In pub, with friends, eating to keep my hands busy.	Why can't she learn to relax with us? She's known us for three years.	They know my quirks and still like me.

While a variety of cognitive and eclectic approaches to social phobia have been used, Butler and Wells conclude that advances in the treatment of social phobia will depend on the development and implementation of a detailed cognitive model, one that can account for the maintenance of the problem, and from which hypotheses concerning potentially effective intervention strategies can be derived and tested. This suggests that while there are certain regularities in social phobia, such as the fact that social phobics in general have assumptions and beliefs that need to be questioned as to their validity, each individual case is different. Therefore, therapists need to guard against falling into formulaic interventions, such as informing the client that his fear is necessarily based on false assumptions. The fact that a phobia is, by definition, based on assumptions and beliefs that are actually untrue does not mean that, in any given case, their untruth has been adequately demonstrated. Thus, merely telling clients that their beliefs are false cannot take the place of disconfirming evidence. This is especially true in the case of social phobia, for social phobics are accustomed to viewing the social world from the perspective of submission. Consequently, their "agreement" with the therapist that their beliefs and assumptions must be false may amount to little more than compliant behavior toward a person who, in this context, is perceived as a member of the dominant class.

Underlying this compliance lies the unstated counter-argument that the therapist experiences the social world as nonthreatening because, "unlike me, he is a healthy, well-adjusted person." The client's assumption that the therapist is a healthy, well-adjusted person may, of course, be in error. Ross (1980) reports that one of the great frustrations of therapists who are also phobic is their success in helping others overcome their phobias, but they are unable to cope effectively with phobias of their own. The main point here, however, is that therapists need to be aware that socially phobic clients may simply "agree" with the therapist because this is their usual way of avoiding social anxiety.

A Case Example of Cognitive-Behavior Treatment

Heimberg and Juster (1994) provide an interesting case example of their treatment program, one that makes considerable use of cognitive restructuring procedures (in conjunction with simulated exposure). A key aspect of this approach is helping clients identify what Beck and his colleagues (1979) call "automatic thoughts." The client, Jack, a forty-seven-year-old with a doctorate in engineering, had been employed for eighteen years as a senior engineer for a large research and manufacturing firm at the time he sought treatment. Married for twenty-five years, he and his wife had two children age twenty-one and eighteen years. By all accounts, he was stable and well-adjusted. He came for treatment, however, with a primary complaint of longstanding fear of public speaking, an important component of his job. Further discussion revealed that he was also concerned about appearing nervous to others in situations involving any type of confrontation or potential for confrontation. Confrontation was broadly defined and could take the form of discussing a controversial issue, finding himself in a situation in which he wished to assert himself, or receiving constructive criticism from his wife or his supervisor. Anticipation of interpersonal conflict provoked strong anxiety.

The diagnostic interview revealed that he met the *DSM-IV* criteria for social phobia, and that his anxiety was markedly disturbing and disabling. Because he reported no difficulty with nonconfrontational social interaction, he did not meet the criteria for the generalized subtype of social phobia, which is applied when a client fears most social situations. In effect, his phobia was essentially situational domain specific, relating primarily to the "assertive interaction" domain. Difficulties in the other interaction domains (both formal and informal), however, were also present. He reported that he responded to confrontation and public speaking situations with a mix of physiological symptoms, including moderate levels of breathing difficulty, accelerated heart rate, and hot flashes, mild levels of chest discomfort and sweating, and occasional trembling. In addition to these symptoms, he reportedly began to experience extreme blushing in front of others after his recovery from a heart attack at age thirty-eight. While he dated the onset of his social phobia to age eighteen, he could identify no specific precipitating event.

The initial sessions with Jack were devoted to education in the cognitive-behavioral model of social phobia, training in the techniques of cognitive restructuring, and helping him become more comfortable speaking in front of other members of the therapy group to which he was assigned. In the first session, he expressed concern that his physiological symptoms, especially blushing, quivering voice, and increased heart rate, would have catastrophic effects on his career. In the second session, he began to identify a fairly common set of automatic thoughts. These included the idea that he would become unbearably nervous and uncomfortable, that his nervousness would be visible to others, that it would interfere with his ability to talk, and that others would think there was something very wrong with him. Further questioning revealed thoughts about being inferior and feeling like an idiot.

His first simulated exposure (session four) involved a conversation with a new coworker during a coffee break at work. While this situation was not directly related to his fears of public speaking or confrontation, it had the potential to elicit an anxious reaction from him because the evaluative aspects of the situation and public nature of the situation were stressed. When presented this scenario, Jack reported several automatic thoughts about the visibility of his anxiety to others. He reported that he would be highly self-conscious and embarrassed. He stated his concern that he would be unable to think of things to say and that the things he did say would not be interesting enough. Consequently, he would not perform up to the standard he set for himself or that others expected from him.

Through group discussion, a number of logical distortions in his automatic thoughts were identified. For example, he had a tendency to engage in dichotomous thinking about his conversational abilities. He thought his topics of conversation were either captivating or sedating. There was nothing in between. This revealed little recognition that topics vary on this dimension and that the same topic might elicit different reactions from different people. Also, he set such a high threshold for a topic to be judged interesting that few topics ever were. He endorsed a number of inflexible and vague rules about how his performance "should be" and applied a very negative label to himself when he could not meet these unrealistic standards ("I'm inferior").

Through further discussion, he was able to confront the illogic in these thoughts. He agreed that he was capable of carrying on a pleasant conversation and that his standards were probably unrealistic. As an alternative response to his concerns that his anxiety would interfere with his performance, he chose the statement, "I can be nervous and carry on a pleasant conversation." He selected the goal of introducing himself to the new coworker, saying four things about himself, and learning three things about the coworker. His goals met the criteria of being observable, measurable, realistic, and task-oriented.

By all accounts, he performed exceedingly well. In addition, during cognitive processing after the conclusion of the exposure, he reported several important observations. First, he saw that he had carried on a conversation while he was the center of attention. Second, he noted that his anxiety declined over time; therefore, feared situations could be managed. He stated that if he could get through the first minute (and he now had evidence that he could), he would be fine. He also reported that it helped that he was required to read his rational response aloud ("I can be nervous and carry on a pleasant conversation") during the exposure itself. It reminded him that despite his anxiety he was actually carrying on a conversation. Other group members also provided much positive feedback. He remained concerned, however, about one instance in which he "drew a blank" and the potential negative impact such pauses might have on how he was evaluated by others. This concern was addressed in later exposures.

By session six, he reported success in completing behavioral homework assignments involving initiating meetings at work and going to lunch with a group of coworkers. For his second simulated exposure, he was asked to talk about himself and his job with two new employees at work. Reflecting the same themes that were present in his first exposure, he reported the automatic thoughts, "I'll go blank," "I'll look nervous," "I should be able to do this," and "I should think of things to say." The final thought was reinterpreted as a problem of knowing the "right" thing to say, another example of dichotomous thinking. To counteract this, the alternative rational responses, "I may be nervous, but I will think of things to say," and "It's okay to take a pause," were developed. His goals for this exposure were to say four things about himself, four things about the job, and purposely pause twice. His response after the exposure was simply, "It went terrific!" While he expected to be much more hesitant and suffer great embarrassment, he received feedback from the group that he did not appear nervous, that his pacing was just right, and that his pauses were appropriate and helped to emphasize certain points. Hearing this feedback, he proclaimed "I can do this!"

Through discussion of homework and previous exposure experiences, he was able to recognize that his concerns about confrontation were related to his discomfort with the expression of anger. For his third exposure in session eight, he was to confront a coworker regarding a problem involving the coworker's performance, something he usually expended great energy to avoid. He developed the rational responses, "I can be angry and still be okay," and "Others can know when I'm angry." Goals for this exposure were to make two comments about the problem and to let the individual know "how he felt," specifically, that he was unhappy with the other person's performance. He was successful during this role-played exposure. Then, in keeping with the theme of confrontation and expressing a dissenting opinion, he was given the task of making a presentation on a controversial topic in the first half of his fourth exposure and to give his opinion and defend it to the group in the latter half. He identified two automatic thoughts unique to the confrontational theme of the situation, "I won't be able to defend my opinion well," and "I'll do it less than perfectly." Following discussion, rational responses were developed for the presentation phase of the exposure ("It's okay to take a pause" and "I don't need to be perfect") and for the discussion phase ("my opinion is as valid as his"). His goals were to make six points, pause three times, and respond to three objections made by the antagonists. He made an extemporaneous speech on the negative impact of the media on violent behavior, societal attitudes toward women, and teen suicide. He met or exceeded all his goals but was disappointed in his performance. He believed he should have paused more than he did and reported that he wanted to pause during the heated discussion but did not do so because of anxiety.

For his fifth and final in-session exposure, he role-played a conversation with two people at a company picnic in which he was to voice his opinion on a controversial topic. In discussion of his automatic thoughts, it became clear that he was extremely concerned about being liked and he believed that confrontation, expressing his opinion, and being assertive would cause people to dislike him. In disputing these thoughts, he developed the rational response that "It's okay to disagree." Goals included initiating the topic, making three comments on his position, and voicing disagreement with the other role-players. The topic he initiated, both current and controversial, was euthanasia for terminally ill patients. He reported that he performed better than he anticipated and that, to his surprise, he felt excited and eager when talking on the subject rather than angry and concerned about how others viewed him. He again met or exceeded all his goals and concluded that talking itself lowers anxiety and increases eagerness.

At the conclusion of treatment, it was recommended that he continue to practice the skills he had learned, focusing specifically on the situations he found most difficult. He had made significant gains as a result of his participation in the cognitive-behavioral group treatment process. While he was able to function at the outset, he had struggled throughout treatment with concerns about being evaluated by others, especially in relation to letting others know when he was angry or wanted to express his opinion. He also employed unrealistic and perfectionist standards to measure outcomes in these difficult situations. By the end of treatment, his anxiety was substantially reduced, and his improvement continued over the course of the one-year follow-up period.

The Use of Paradoxical Interventions

The treatment method developed by Heimberg and colleagues and illustrated by the case of Jack is primarily based on simulated exposure followed by cognitive restructuring. There are, however, many other behavioral-cognitive methods. For example, Marks (1995) describes a realtively new method developed by Newell and Shrubb (1994) termed "paradoxical role-play." This method involves having the therapist take the position that the client's negative beliefs about himself are actually true and placing the client in the position of having to argue that they are actually untrue. This technique is illustrated by a client whose social phobia was mainly due to the belief that his body was terribly misshapen, with head and torso much too large. In presenting the client with the role-play assignment, Marks was explicit about what he hoped would be the outcome of their role-play. He said to the client: "You believe that your head and torso are grotesquely large and that this is the truth. This might, however, be a matter of opinion. Why don't you carry out an experiment with me?" He went on to note that what we believe is strengthened by what we say aloud to ourselves or what we rehearse in our minds. We practice our beliefs just as we practice playing the piano or tennis. Since therapist and client agree that the client's rehearsing and acting on his beliefs greatly handicaps his life, the experiment will involve the client practicing saying alternative beliefs purely to feel what it is like to say and think these things rather than what he has been saying and thinking until now. In proposing that they would engage in debate, Marks emphasized that the client did not have to believe that what he was saying was true, that all he needed to do was to argue it passionately as if he did.

Conducted as if it were a scene in court, the role-play lasted twenty minutes the first week and twenty minutes the following week. It consisted of exchanges between the therapist and client like the following:

Therapist: You deny in front of the court that your head doesn't touch the walls when you turn it?

Client: Yes, several feet of space come in between.

Therapist: In that case, the prosecution alleges that your head is so big that you could never wear a hat.

Client: That is not true! I have worn several hats in the past and have photographs to prove it!

Therapist: Ah, but you had them specially tailor-made for outsized heads.

Client: No, I bought them in normal department stores like everyone else.

This approach was so successful that by the time therapy was concluded, the client's negative self-beliefs were greatly reduced in intensity and frequency. Upon follow-up eighteen months later, the belief had practically disappeared.

Marks acknowledges that the positive results of this role-play may have been aided by concurrent exposure tasks, including one in which the client wore shorts and a T-shirt while talking with women, a task devised by the client himself. Thus, while this case illustrates how unconditional beliefs about the self may be undermined, it also demonstrates the value of challenging a client's conditional beliefs about social evaluation. As his self-belief changed ("I'm not abnormal"), his anticipation of negative evaluation by others was also revised.

As Newell and Shrubb indicate, paradox is the key feature of this role-playing method. The paradox is that the therapist "agrees" with the phobic person and the phobic person assumes the role of the "rational" critic of his false assumptions or beliefs. The therapeutic uses of paradox are not the creation of cognitive-behavioral therapists, however, but are attributable to Viktor Frankl, who used paradox in his psychotherapeutic work as early as 1929 and published a paper on "paradoxical intention" a decade later (Frankl 1939). Frankl applied paradoxical intention to phobias because this technique is based on the premise that the vicious cycle of anticipatory anxiety may be broken by replacing the client's pathogenic fear with a paradoxical wish. A deliberate attempt to faint will relax a person to such a degree that fainting becomes the one thing she cannot do. In Frankl's view, paradoxical intention utilizes or mobilizes a coping mechanism wired into each and every human being (1975). He does not explain the source of this mechanism, but implies that it is biological.

Lukas (1984), a therapist trained in Frankl's therapeutic method, illustrates how the paradoxical method might be used in the case of a social phobic (79–81). Suppose a teenaged apprentice is suddenly called to his boss's office. Because of the excitement, or even because the room is warm, he perspires and the boss makes a seemingly harmless remark about it. The next time the apprentice is called to the boss's office the boy becomes afraid he may perspire again. He carefully wipes his face, enters the office, and the fear of perspiring drives the sweat from his pores. After the second experience he is certain that the third time he faces the boss he will be dripping with sweat. His anticipatory anxiety increases and is confirmed every time. He tries to run away from it, avoids the boss's office, calls in sick when he expects to be summoned, takes tranquilizers, and gets caught more and more in a desperate cycle. His anxiety spreads to other situations. He fears he may sweat when talking to any grown-up; he withdraws, becomes a loner, his shyness increases, and he finds less courage to face people. He sees a doctor who prescribes new tranquilizers. The boss cannot use an apprentice who gets sick so often and so he fires him. This failure throws the young man even more into the grip of fear. He develops a general fear of life, his self-confidence diminishes, his body is affected and produces, in addition to perspiration, palpitations of the heart and sleep disturbances, and one day the young man is "finished."

How would paradoxical therapy help this young man avoid this fate? First, he is encouraged, using humorous formulations, to intend exactly what he fears, namely sweating. He learns to tell himself that he must show his boss just how much he can sweat. He imagines perspiring a puddle in the boss's office so the boss would drown in it. This would be a good way to get rid of the boss, as well as his fear of him. Lukas explains that the formulations sound exaggerated because they *must* sound exaggerated enough so that they won't work as auto-suggestions. Only when the formulations are ridiculous enough is it possible for the patient not to take them seriously. The purpose of this technique is to bring clients to the point where they will not take the formulations and their whole unfounded fear seriously. In effect, the formulations function as a "go-between." The client's attitude toward the formulations is transferred to his attitude toward his emotional disorder. The more exaggerated and ridiculous the formulations, the more exaggerated and ridiculous the phobia seems. The neurotic cycle is broken, the fear is deprived of its power, the consequences of the fear are reduced, and new phobic attacks become less likely. The vicious cycle is reversed in the direction of the client's health.

Lukas also notes that the reduction of symptoms in this case is achieved gradually. The apprentice realizes that he is unable to perspire even when he tries hard, the fear loses its terror, he begins to laugh about it, and the specter disappears. She acknowledges that this method has its critics who argue that the danger with paradoxical intention is the possible spreading of the symptoms. Because the deep-seated causes of the existing symptoms are not sufficiently unearthed, other symptoms will simply replace the old. She disagrees with this line of reasoning. Regardless of whether or not a deep-seated cause is present, the existing symptom itself becomes the cause of a chain of new symptoms. However they are caused, phobias bring about a lower self-image, a pattern of avoidance, a withdrawal from activities, and often the conviction of being a complete failure. Recall the woman priest in this regard. She has come to believe that her success as a priest depends on her ability to hold the chalice without spilling. Therefore, Lukas contends that therapists cannot afford to disregard the present symptoms and to search for imagined or suspected causes while valuable time slips by and a new chain of symptoms is formed. The deeper causes can always be explored later if necessary, but first the chain of unhappy consequences must be interrupted; the symptoms must be reduced. When this is accomplished, positive feedback reactions bring new confidence and help clients overcome and cope with any deeper causes that may exist.

Akillas and Efran (1995), however, have recently raised a different criticism of symptom prescription. In their study, the effects of two types of paradoxical directives on a group of socially phobic men were evaluated. The first method was "symptom prescription," such as instructing a person to tremble at a social gathering. The other involved "reframing," which consists of attempting to change the meaning that clients attribute to problematic behavior, such as encouraging a client to perceive the symptoms as desirable or amusing. Reframing advocates contend that symptom prescription is effective because it implicitly "reframes" the behavior by transforming a client's perception of the symptom from negative to positive (see Watzlawick et al. 1974). The Akillas and Efran study predicted that the effects of paradoxical directives are mediated by changes in the meaning clients attribute to their symptoms. It further predicted that prescribing symptoms would be therapeutic if it suggested to the client that the problematic behaviors are not as pathological and handicapping as he thinks they are. In other words, without introducing modifications in the way symptoms are perceived, paradoxical directives will not be effective in producing therapeutic changes. Thus, reframing is the key element of paradoxical psychotherapy.

The paradoxical directives were applied in three weekly individual sessions and were based on information obtained from subjects during the first session regarding the difficulties they experienced in social situations and their previous attempts to remedy them. All subjects were asked to perform the very behavior that they would normally attempt to avoid or to "fix." For example, a person concerned about being silent at a party was instructed to avoid talking at a social event unless he felt he had something important to communicate. In one group of subjects, symptom prescription was used without reframing. In the other, it was used with reframing. In the former group, the therapist would preface the symptom prescription with the statement, "I am going to ask you to do something *strange but helpful* for the next two weeks," and would then instruct him to do the very things he had been trying to avoid doing. The authors call this "symptom prescription without reframing" because the subject is asked to follow these "illogical" injunctions on faith, without trying to understand the rationale behind them. In the second group, the therapist gave the subject the following rationale: that socializing should happen spontaneously and only when it feels good; that his efforts to overcome anxiety had probably made socializing a burden; that the choice about whether or not he should socialize in a given situation needs to belong to him; that he has the right *not* to socialize if it does not feel good to him; and that the assignment will help him to discover how it feels when he chooses not to do things that do not feel good. In other words, "the therapist reframed the problematic behaviors as legitimate choices, and suggested that they should be practiced and explored in that spirit" (268).

On the basis of questionnaire and self-rating scales on anxiety, avoidance, and inhibition, the authors concluded that symptom prescription with reframing is much more effective than symptom prescription without it. Especially noteworthy was the discovery that the group receiving reframing reported a much earlier and persisting decrease in inhibition than the other group. These results support the authors' contention that socially phobic persons are helped by symptom prescription "if it enables clients to view their symptoms as legitimate and nonpathological behaviors" (277). What gets "reframed" is the client's view that it is somehow wrong or bad to want to avoid socializing, or public speaking, or whatever her particular phobia may be. Also, if she decides not to socialize, give a talk, or speak with a person in authority, this is her legitimate choice. In other words, the underlying assumption of the reframing method in this particular study is that the client has relinquished personal choice regarding social situations that are in fact matters of personal choice. The reframing approach encourages her to recover the personal autonomy, the right to govern her own life, that is rightfully hers.

Conclusion

Because it is now the most widely used approach with social phobics, much more could be said here about the cognitive-behavioral treatment method. However, this relatively brief account indicates that the key issue for cognitive-behavioral therapists is whether the social phobic's fear of a given social situation is, in fact, justified. By definition *(DSM-IV)*, a phobia has its basis in fears that are "excessive" or "unreasonable." (The more pejorative word "irrational" is no longer used.) Cognitive-behavioral therapists do not wish to challenge this basic understanding of what a phobia is. On the other hand, by making the cognitions of the social phobic primary, they have opened up the whole issue of whether or to what extent the fear is warranted. As a basic strategy, they seek to help the social phobic recognize that his fear is not supported by the available evidence, or at least that there are alternative ways of viewing the situation, calling into question the validity of his assumptions and beliefs. The study by Akillas and Efran (1995) suggests, however, that in any given instance the question of whether the social phobic's view of the feared social situation is actually justified is not an easy one to answer. To be sure, they couch this issue in terms of the individual's right to exercise personal choice; therefore, they do not directly address the question whether or not the fear itself is justified. And yet, they certainly challenge the common assumption that the goal of therapy is always to help individuals engage in the feared social situation with a greater degree of comfort. Their reframing approach indicates that this may not be the appropriate therapeutic goal in some instances, and that the more significant goal may be to assist the client in recognizing that she may exercise personal choice in the matter and need not feel ashamed, weak, or inferior if the choice is to avoid the situation. Thus, negative unconditional beliefs about the self may be decreased even as the individual continues to *avoid* certain feared social situations. We may relate this reframing of the social phobic's fear to Öhman's dominance/submissiveness issue, because it suggests that a person may have justifiable grounds for avoiding a social situation in which his very presence would support or reinforce the power of the "dominant class" against him. In such situations, the social phobic's fear of the situation is neither excessive nor unreasonable. On the contrary, to enter into such situations may be to act against his own self-interests and may even be self-destructive. Paradoxically, it *could* be a form of masochism or even self-abuse.

CHAPTER 6

Psychotherapeutic Treatment Methods

All of the treatment methods discussed thus far are psychotherapeutic in that they are psychologically, not pharmacologically, focused. There are some therapists, however, for whom psychotherapy is the primary, even exclusive method of treatment. They believe that social phobics can be helped by talking about their phobia, on a one-to-one basis, with a trained, sympathetic listener. They also feel that the techniques employed by other therapists (such as exposure, social skills training, cognitive restructuring, symptom prescription) are not necessarily more effective than exploration of a client's reflections on how she acquired the phobia and factors that contribute to its continuing persistence. While other methods were developed, in part, because the standard psychotherapeutic approach was considered ineffective with social phobia, the fact that no single method is considered significantly more effective with all types of social phobics leads some therapists to claim that psychotherapy is not necessarily inferior to treatment methods specifically developed for social phobia, and that for some clients it is the preferred approach.

One basic assumption of psychotherapy is that the social phobia needs to be viewed in relation to all the other problems and difficulties that clients are experiencing. The social phobia should not be treated in isolation from these other personal problems. Progress on the social phobia is most likely to be made when there is corresponding progress with these other problems. This assumption is based on the fact that many individuals who seek psychotherapy do not cite social phobia as their reason for seeking treatment. As Zerbe points out, clients "with social phobia complain of a plethora of other psychiatric problems that often take precedence in formal diagnostic reports and treatment planning" (1994, A6). Social phobia often goes undiagnosed or is minimized in the diagnostic assessment because other conditions are felt to be more prominent, preoccupying, or life threatening, such as alcoholism, depression, or anorexia.

Another basic assumption is that it is not enough to focus on removing the symptoms (e.g., the inability to attend a social gathering without experiencing severe anxiety). This is because the symptoms are likely to persist or return if the underlying cause of the phobia is not identified. As Menninger (1994) points out, a persistent and careful search usually enables the therapist to identify a precipitating incident or conflict. If this incident is effectively addressed, the need for additional treatment or medication may be markedly reduced. Often the patient may have a strong psychological reason to deny the incident or conflict and to avoid seeing the link between exacerbation of the anxiety disorder and the precipitating event. Thus, the key feature of therapy "may be a symbolic reexperiencing or association with an intitial trauma, which often is related to a disrupted relationship or present or past abuse" by an important person in the client's life (A88). While the psychoanalytic form of psychotherapy is the most concerned to make this point that the phobia is symbolic of an initial trauma, most psychotherapists believe that the phobia is rooted in past events or current relationships and that these need to be identified and explored with the client. They are not content to treat the client's current anxiety without such exploration.

In a clinical report advocating a rapprochement between behavioral and psychotherapeutic approaches to phobias, Llewelyn notes that when one works from a psychotherapeutic orientation, it is "axiomatic that symptoms are not taken at face value" (1980, 145). Thus, when a client complains of having a phobia, the psychotherapist probes the complaint in depth until an underlying cause or present relationship difficulty is identified. She cautions, however, that this approach may need to be modified in the case of *social* phobia for three important reasons. One is that the patient may be totally unaware of such underlying causes, so that many explanatory discussions will not reveal or unearth them. A second is that the symptoms may exist because the basic difficulties are far too uncomfortable to face, leading to the building of a defense system that even sensitive exploration cannot penetrate. A third is that even if the therapist were to persist and succeed with the exploration, the habitual remnants of the presenting symptoms may continue to reduce the opportunities for new ways of behaving and relating in light of the newly acquired insights.

Thus, she proposes that the psychotherapist focus on the presenting symptoms in the beginning stages of the psychotherapeutic relationship and then move to the deeper issues as the opportunity presents itself. To illustrate, she reports the case of a thirty-five year old steel worker who came to see her because he reacted phobically (clammy hands, heart palpitations, urge to urinate) when his ear was pricked with a needle during the biannual lead test performed at work. This problem had been magnified by the kidding he received from his workmates about his being afraid of "a little needle." When he came to see Llewelyn, he hadn't worked for three months, despite the fact that he "loved" his work and nothing else about his job caused him any distress.

Llewelyn's approach was initially behavioral as she taught him a standard relaxation procedure. Desensitization was also employed. This involved having him enter the testing room at work and in a series of graduated steps working up to standing in the line of men and joking about the lead test. Because he also reported having had a fear of dentists since childhood and had not gone to one in ten years, a similar desensitization plan was employed to eliminate his fear of dentists. After he went to the dentist for extensive, long-delayed dental work, he declared that he had "climbed a mountain," and decided he would return to work the following week. As he saw it, in comparison with going to the dentist, the lead test now seemed rather insignificant. While Llewelyn does not make this association, the dentist scenario may be viewed as an example of the reframing technique of "providing a worse alternative" (Haley 1973, 25–26).

He returned to work and reported the complete remission of his fear of the lead test. He took the next test on schedule and proclaimed that, as far as he was concerned, the treatment had been a complete success. A three-month follow-up was scheduled. However, one month later he phoned Llewelyn, requesting urgent help. He came to the session with his wife and reported that he was no longer going to work and was "afraid of everything." Concurring, his wife reported that he had spent his day off driving aimlessly around town. He explained that this was due to panic feelings about the prospect of another lead test. Several counseling sessions were held, during which he continued to talk about his fears of returning to work. Then, at their request, joint sessions were held with the man and his wife, during which it became clear that there were deep marital problems. As these sessions continued, Llewelyn became convinced that the fear of the lead test at work was a substitute for his fear of the real problem, his troubled marriage. The lead test subsided into a minor worry and therapy focused instead on exploration and examination of his guilt, distress, and anxiety about making a decision to leave his wife and to face life as an independent individual.

The next month, after missing two consecutive counseling sessions, he came and announced that he had left his wife and was returning to work that week. At the following session he reported that he had attended marriage guidance sessions with his wife but was not intending to reconsider his decision to leave her. He said that he had organized his finances and was providing adequately for her and the children. In subsequent sessions he reported continued satisfaction in his new life as a single man. While sad at the loss of his children, he was resolute in his belief that he had done the right thing both for himself and his wife by abandoning "a hopeless marriage." At the follow-up session scheduled four months later, he appeared with an earring in his ear. He had voluntarily submitted to a procedure, for the sake of fashion, that previously terrified him so much that he had been off work for nine months. The lead test no longer held any fear for him, he was re-establishing a social life for himself, and was pleased that his wife was also beginning to accept the new situation. He attributed the success of the treatment to recognition of his fundamental dissatisfaction with his marriage and viewed the lead test phobia as a substitute for a more basic difficulty. He added, however, that if Llewelyn had suggested to him that the lead test phobia was symptomatic of something deeper, he would not have "bothered to consider it seriously."

Llewelyn believes that this case illustrates the importance of working with what is presented by the client rather than insisting that he be dealt with according to a predetermined treatment plan. She also believes that it supports the emphasis in recent research on the importance of "non-specific factors" in therapy, as the constant element throughout all phases of the treatment was the therapeutic relationship itself. In her view, it was this relationship, together with "non-specific factors such as commitment, hope, and attention," that allowed the process of change to occur.

In a study that supports Llewelyn's position, Hand and Lamontagne (1976) found an unexpectedly high rate of acute interpersonal crises after successful treatment of agoraphobia and social phobia by group exposure. Twenty-one of the twenty-five individuals studied (mean age: 35; mean symptom duration: eight and one-half years) were married. Fourteen of the married clients were aware of chronic marital problems before the treatment began, but all regarded their phobia as far more crippling. Thus they wanted phobia therapy rather than the marital therapy that was offered as an alternative. Immediately or soon after the phobia was successfully treated, however, six of the fourteen who had regarded their marriage as unsatisfactory and one of the seven who had not complained about her marriage before treatment had such acute crises in their marital relationships that they either asked for or were again offered marital therapy. Only three of the seven couples, however, entered into joint marital therapy. Two patients refused it, as did two spouses.

The authors provide several case illustrations. For example, as one of the client's phobia improved, he became depressed, agitated, and paranoid not only toward his wife but also toward policemen (the latter being connected with some obscure feelings of guilt). A few sessions sufficed to calm him down, after which the couple had several joint marital therapy sessions. After some changes in their home environment, they got along much better than before. At this point, however, he relapsed into his phobia of going out, giving as a reason his paranoid feelings about policemen. With supportive therapy, these feelings disappeared, but he now felt increasingly dependent on his wife and relapsed even more into his phobia, giving his "old" reason of a fear of dying from a heart attack.

Another patient mentioned marital problems in the assessment interview. These problems were partly due to her husband's position in the Navy, which she hated but he was reluctant to give up. Her phobia developed after his decision to remain in the Navy and their move to a city that she disliked. She improved during treatment and remained symptom-free afterwards. However, at the three-month follow-up, which was to be her last meeting with the therapist, she asked for a discussion of her marital problems. Being an illegitimate child, she had always been warned by her stepparents not to become promiscuous like her mother. Thus, she came to hate her natural mother but felt guilty about this after her mother's death. She had been pushed into marriage by her stepparents. She liked her husband because of his personality, though she could hardly ever get sexual satisfaction. In the new city, she felt easily arousable by certain men and women, which made her feel afraid of her sexuality and reminded her of her stepparents' warning about her promiscuous mother. During the interview she was desperate about the situation and wanted either significant changes in her marriage or a new beginning on her own. Joint marital therapy was offered but her husband refused.

While fourteen of the twenty-one married clients mentioned marital problems in the assessment interview, the authors were unable to find any consistent pattern of interaction between phobic symptoms and interpersonal problems, especially with regard to what effect a phobia or its rapid removal might have on chronic marital problems. In half of the fourteen cases where clients were aware of marital problems, phobia removal was not followed by an acute crisis and sometimes actually led to improvements in their marriage. Moreover, when the therapist and client both recognized that marital problems were involved, clients always insisted on phobia treatment rather than marital therapy. Like Llewelyn, the authors suggest that it is best to accede to the client's wishes in this regard, because in some cases the marital problems were significantly reduced when the phobia was successfully treated, while in other cases the successful treatment of the phobia led clients whose marital situations worsened to request marital therapy.

These studies indicate that phobias are sometimes related to marital problems and that phobic symptoms may be a consequence of these problems. To address the phobic symptomology without also addressing the deeper, underlying marital problems may lead to a premature declaration of therapeutic success. In the studies cited, however, it was not until the phobia was successfully treated that the client was able to face the underlying issues. Admittedly, the Llewelyn study focused on a specific phobia (fear of needle penetration) and most, though not all, of the clients in the Hand and Lamontagne study (1976) were diagnosed as agoraphobics. A case study of a social phobic (Humphreys and Beiman 1975), however, reveals the same combination of phobic behavior (including difficulty in speaking before an audience, sitting in church and going to restaurants, and confronting an authority figure) and marital difficulties. In this case the phobia was successfully treated with behavioral techniques, but the marital problems persisted and proved impervious to behavioral treatment methods. The client's spouse refused joint marital therapy. Interestingly enough, one of the authority figures the client had difficulty confronting was his father-in-law. (His church phobia was counteracted by having him move one pew forward on successive Sundays until he was sitting in the front row without anxiety.)

Thus, the relationship between phobia and current marital difficulties applies to social phobics as well, and the same complex relationship between therapeutic success with the phobia and improvement or lack of improvement in the marriage relationship is also present. This does not mean, of course, that marital difficulties underlie all social phobias. These cases, however, support the theory that phobias have underlying causes or precipitating environmental features, and they indicate that the social phobic may be helped by exploration of these causes and precipitating factors.

The Psychoanalytic Approach to Social Phobia

Thus far we have focused on the possible relationship between social phobia and current interpersonal problems, especially marital problems. The psychoanalytic perspective on social phobia asserts, however, that social phobia is more likely caused by childhood emotional trauma than by current interpersonal difficulties. This view has a better fit with the typical age of onset of social phobia, usually in adolescence, in most instances prior to marriage as well as current work relationships. This view is also supported by the fact that many social phobics attribute their phobia problems to inadequate or idiosyncratic parenting. Thus, while we would expect psychotherapists with a psychoanalytic orientation to focus on early childhood experiences because this is what they do with all of their patients, there may be especially valid grounds for doing so in the case of social phobics. From this viewpoint, the current marital or other interpersonal difficulties cited by other psychotherapists would be considered symptomatic of even deeper interpersonal problems going back to early childhood. The case reported by Hand and Lamontagne of the woman whose marital problems may be traced to guilt feelings relating to her "promiscuous" mother support this psychoanalytic position.

In an essay on the psychodynamics of panic disorder and social phobia, Gabbard (1992) presents the psychoanalytic view of social phobia. He cites the studies of shy or behaviorally inhibited children by Kagan (1986/1987) and his colleagues, noting that they provide strong evidence of a temperamental risk factor for social phobia. He also notes, however, that Kagan and his team concluded that some form of chronic environmental stress must act on the original temperamental disposition present at birth to result in shy, timid, and quiet behavior at two years of age. Kagan et al. postulated such environmental stresses as humiliation and criticism from an older sibling, parental arguments, and the death of or separation from a parent. Gabbard suggests, however, that the major environmental stress behind future social phobia is the mother-child relationship. While this is the predictable argument from psychoanalytically oriented theorists regarding any future emotional disorder, certain symptoms of social phobia seem to provide support for it.

In Gabbard's view, the basic assumption of psychoanalysis is that the symptoms of social phobia may be understood as compromise formations between expressions of unacceptable wishes and fantasies on the one hand and defenses against those wishes and fantasies on the other. Because certain key developmental experiences are kept alive in the symptomatology, these experiences may provide clues as to what forms of chronic interaction with persons in the environment are particularly relevant. He notes specifically that shame experiences often underlie social phobia: "The underlying unconscious wish of these patients is to be the center of attention and to receive affirming responses from others. This wish automatically produces a sense of being shamed or censured by disapproving parental figures. To avoid this imagined humiliation or embarrassment, victims of social phobia simply avoid situations where they risk such disapproving reactions from others" (A8). This shame/avoidance dynamic is rooted in the fact that the infant *is* the center of attention in the earliest months of life and becomes accustomed to it. Psychoanalysts refer to this as "primary narcissism." "Secondary narcissism" occurs when the infant loses center-of-attention status or is ill treated, feels shamed by this loss, and uses manipulative efforts to regain his earlier, privileged status. Thus, Gabbard suggests that phobias that involve avoidant behaviors have their roots in the shaming experiences of secondary narcissism (see also Bergmann 1980).

Gabbard argues that guilt feelings may also play a pivotal role in the symptoms of social phobia. Some social phobics have an unconscious desire for complete attention from others, and this desire is manifest in an aggressive wish to scare away all rivals for another person's attention. In turn, these aggressive wishes cause the social phobic to feel guilty, especially because the demand for the undivided, exclusive attention of the other is patently unreasonable. Gabbard suggests that these guilt feelings are often interwoven with a sense of shame stemming from the feeling that one is not really capable of displacing rivals and is therefore fraudulent or deceptive. Here Gabbard is invoking the psychoanalytic Oedipal theory, which emphasizes the male child's rivalry with his father for his mother's attentions. The same argument, however, may also apply to the female child's rivalry with her mother for her father's attentions. In either case, there are significant parallels here between Gabbard's psychoanalytic perspective and Öhman's theory that social phobia is rooted in the dominance/submissiveness dynamics of human interaction. Especially noteworthy in this regard is Gabbard's view that there is an aggressive substratum that underlies social phobia, and that such aggression pertains to the social phobic's sensitivity to the existence of rivals for a loved one's attentions. This rivalry, however, may apply not only to the child's feelings about the same-sex parent but also to siblings who are also vying for one or the other parent's attentions.

Gabbard suggests that a third dynamic found in social phobia is separation anxiety. This anxiety develops when the child fears that his efforts to become autonomous and connected to others will result in losing his primary caregiver's love. This is where the mother-child relationship comes to be viewed by psychoanalytically-oriented therapists as a major environmental factor in social phobia. In their studies of mother-infant pairs, Mahler and colleagues (1975) have observed sudden anxious reactions in children related to a fear that mother had left the room when, in fact, she had not moved from her chair at all. They conclude that the desire to be autonomous and to separate from mother raises fears that she may wish to leave the child. In support of this conclusion, they point to their observations of a frequent tendency for the mother to become irritated and to react negatively to her child's striving for autonomy. If these developmental fears are reinforced by excessively rejecting behavior from parents or caregivers, children may grow up with the sense that any move toward autonomy will result in abandonment. As adults, these persons may feel that they can forestall catastrophic cutoffs from nurturing figures by avoiding any connection or engagement with persons in the outside world.

Gabbard argues that all three of these dynamics—shame/avoidance, guilt/aggression, and separation anxiety/autonomy seeking—are a reflection of certain characteristic internal object-representations, including parents, caregivers, or siblings who shame, criticize, ridicule, humiliate, abandon, and embarrass the small child. These introjects are established early in life and are repeatedly projected onto persons in the environment who are then avoided. He believes that there may be a genetic predisposition to experience others in this manner. Therefore, to the extent that "caregivers behave in a manner similar to the programmed template, the individual will become increasingly fearful of others and develop social phobia" (A9). Conversely, to the extent that caregivers are sensitive to the child's fearfulness and make compensations for it, the introjects will be more benign, less threatening, and less likely to produce a full-blown case of social phobia. Because the social phobia develops and is maintained by means of these internal object-representations, the phobia is, in effect, an internal one. This is why a phobic's fear may be considered to be excessive and unreasonable, a key *DSM-IV* criterion for a social phobia diagnosis. That is, it is greater than external circumstances—for example, threats—actually warrant.

As far as psychoanalytic treatment is concerned, Gabbard notes that Freud advocated exposure to the anxiety-arousing situation. This was not because he believed that the phobia would thereby be extinguished (as behavioral therapy asserts) but because doing so would help the patient become aware of the underlying conflicts that precipitated and continue to maintain the phobia. Gabbard suggests that the decision to use psychotherapy alone or to combine it with behavioral techniques (such as exposure) depends largely on the characteristics of the patient. For the patient who is psychologically-minded and is curious about the unconscious factors that contribute to the symptomatology, psychotherapy may be the preferred choice even though it may not ultimately be the least expensive form of treatment. But whatever approach one uses, Gabbard emphasizes that the therapist needs to be aware of the patient's tendency to "transfer" negative or critical introjects onto the therapist. Socially phobic patients anticipate that they will be censured or abandoned for being assertive or for expressing themselves in ways that could be construed as reflecting excessive self-regard. In turn, therapists need to be aware of their own counter-transference responses. The reticence and inhibition of these patients may evoke a response of impatience and irritation that serves to confirm their fears. As these anxieties emerge, however, they can be systematically interpreted to make the patient increasingly aware of her unconscious concerns. Furthermore, the therapeutic situation "provides an ideal form for presenting a more appropriate object relationship to be internalized by the patient" (A10). As the patient recognizes that the therapist is a concerned and empathic person who is not interested in humiliating or shaming him, he begins to internalize a selfobject interaction that modifies the highly critical introjects of his internal object world. In this way, his internal object relations are modified through the therapeutic relationship. Gabbard concludes that the "psychodynamic approach not only restores meaning to the symptoms experienced by these patients, but it also has the potential to explicate the ingrained relational patterns that are the source of so much torment in their lives" (A10).

Thus, the psychoanalytic approach does not necessarily involve exposure to the feared situations. Also, unlike the cognitive approach, it does not focus on the patient's misconceptions of the external situation. Instead, its focus is discerning what precipitated the phobia in childhood and how it continues to be maintained as a consequence of the internalization of object-representations. In effect, this approach places considerable emphasis on feared *persons* rather than on feared situations, as these persons are first introjected and then projected onto persons in the social environment who are then avoided. This approach is therefore consistent with the fact that many social phobics experience difficulty in speaking to persons in authority, that is, persons onto whom they project negative object-representations associated with parents, early caregivers, older siblings, and so forth. The fact that social phobics have difficulty asserting themselves, and are unusually sensitive to the dominance/submissiveness dynamics in the social situation, may also be attributed to the aggression they experienced as children against a rival (e.g., same-sex parent or older sibling). As a result of the guilt feelings that this aggression evoked, plus the shame stemming from feelings that one is not really capable of displacing rivals, inhibition of aggression in the form of excessive nonassertiveness may have resulted. In these and other ways, the social phobia is dynamically rooted in early intense interpersonal relationships.

Gabbard's contention that negative internal object-representations are key to social phobia gains some support from a series of empirical studies by Öhman and Dimberg (Öhman 1986). They discovered that when subjects were conditioned to pictures of human faces expressing anger, happiness, and a neutral emotionality, "the angry faces showed much more resistance to extinction than responses to happy or neutral expressions" (135). They found that this effect was amazingly specific. It was obtained only when the stimulus person directed his anger toward the subject. Angry faces looking away had the same effect as happy faces. This suggests that the internal object-representations that are most associated with social phobia are those that evoked fear in the child because the other person was angry at him. This also indicates that psychoanalytic treatment of social phobics should give particular attention to introjects that have an "angry face." Adult social phobia is probably caused less by a mother's insistence on keeping her child close to her and more by her overt expression of anger toward him for his disapproved behavior.

This may also mean that if separation anxiety *is* a cause of adult phobia, it is more likely that the phobia will be agoraphobia, not social phobia. A psychoanalytic study by Coleman (1982/1983) of an agoraphobic patient supports the view that separation anxiety in childhood is related to agoraphobia in adulthood. It concerns a woman whose mother supervised every aspect of her life on the premise that she was a weak, sickly child who might at any moment be carried away by a fatal illness. In the course of treatment for agoraphobia, it emerged that her mother's mother had died six months after the patient's birth. Coleman concludes that the genesis and dynamics of her agoraphobia should be viewed primarily as a result of separation-individuation problems that could not be overcome because of special realities created by her mother's needs. This conclusion is consistent with the common observation that agoraphobics prefer always to be in the company of a trustworthy companion and that they experience great anxiety when venturing out from a "safe place."

That the phobia in this case was agoraphobic, not social phobia, is noteworthy. This suggests that the other dynamics that Gabbard identifies (shame/avoidance and guilt/aggression) are probably more relevant than separation anxiety to social phobia. In other words, the major dynamics in social phobia are (1) the wish to be the center of attention (with corresponding shame for having this wish); and (2) the aggressive demand for attention (with corresponding guilt for the aggression and shame stemming from feelings that one is incapable of displacing the rival for attention). Both dynamics dispose the child toward an avoidance of self-display, even when her desire to be the center of attention for significant accomplishments is altogether appropriate. We are reminded here of the woman who was unable to appear at a company dinner banquet where she was to receive an award for outstanding performance. When she missed the dinner, claiming to be ill, she was invited by her more immediate colleagues to a smaller reception in her honor, which prompted her to quit her job the preceding day in order to avoid being the center of attention (Uhde et al. 1991). Quite possibly, she had learned as a child that being the center of attention was an inappropriate risk. She may also have perceived that this desire had an aggressive aspect to it (i.e., the desire to replace a rival, perhaps an older sibling, as the center of attention).

Meissner et al. (1987) develop the theme of aggression in the genesis of phobias in greater detail than Gabbard. They indicate that the role of aggression in the formation of phobic symptoms and phobic states is a well-established psychoanalytic finding. The psychoanalytic position has been that phobia formations are involved in defending against both libidinal and aggressive impulses, and that the root of fear is not fear of an external object but anxiety regarding one's internal drives. The mechanisms that produce the phobia are meant to contain the anxiety within manageable limits so that the internal danger does not become traumatic. Thus, "oral sadistic impulses to bite or devour can be transformed into fears of being bitten, sadomasochistic wishes to be beaten and tortured can take the form of fears of dark streets or other fears of attack or destruction, and murderous wishes against the oedipal father can become animal phobias" (458).

While Meissner et al. accept this general picture of phobia formation, they object to the common assumption that aggression is an instinctual given. They argue instead that it is motivated and therefore arises only under appropriate stimulus or motivational conditions. The aggression typically develops in the interplay of opposing forces, either involving the child's relationship to one parent, as when she experiences love and hostility toward the same parent, or involving both parents, as when he becomes anxious that if he expresses love toward one parent, the other will become angry, leading to the loss of the angry parent. Thus, a phobia is a symptom indicating intrapsychic conflict, and its manifest affect is fear. The feared object, however, is not dynamically significant in itself, but as an object of symbolic displacement and an externalization of an intolerable mental and conflictual content. The phobia is a compromise formation that makes this psychic situation relatively more tolerable. The creation of the phobia provides safety in this situation by displacing and externalizing one of the conflictful contents. Hence, the external threat is not the significant danger. It only appears to be the source or cause of threat. The dangers that contribute to the formation of a phobia are entirely intrapsychic.

In this view, aggression plays a major role in the development of certain phobias. The aggression in this case needs to be viewed, however, as not only the effort to overcome an external obstacle, whether a person, thing, or situation, but as an attempt to overcome internal psychic obstacles. The phobia displaces the aggression into an apparently innocent object, attributing prior aggression to it. Thus, the aggressive wish persists in relation to the object of displacement, which now has to be avoided. The phobia usually occurs after other alternatives have failed, including repressing the aggression and projecting it onto the other person (i.e., the parent). A phobia emerges as the end result of a progressive narrowing of choices, and it reflects the need both to fulfill a variety of unmanageable wishes and to locate them externally to the self. In this way, even when the phobia elicits intense anxiety, "the sense of self is protected and self-equilibrium is maintained" (475).

The Meissner et al. argument is supported by the fact that social phobics have an excessive fear of being negatively critiqued in social situations. The very excessiveness of the fear indicates that the phobic's own aggression is being projected onto the phobic object (in this case, the social group). While their study focuses mainly on cases of specific phobia and agoraphobia and does not explicitly address social phobia, it provides a theoretical basis for Gabbard's contention that aggression plays a significant role in the development and persistence of social phobia. It also has important implications for treatment of social phobia. Treatment would need to help patients discover that their own aggressions have been externalized. The patient's acceptance of this interpretation would require the therapist's assurance that the original aggression was not innate but was caused by her efforts not to lose a parent's loving attentions. That is, the aggression was perfectly understandable. Since a child cannot live without parental (or caretaker) love, the aggression was for purposes of self-survival. As Meissner et al. indicate, the phobia carefully protects the individual's sense of self.

This suggests, in turn, that if the phobia itself is relinquished, something needs to take its place so that one does not lose the vital sense of self that the phobia, in its own way, has supported. Gabbard's view that the patient needs to experience the therapist as a concerned and empathic person is relevant here, but I also believe that the patient needs something more permanent than this. I will return to this point when I discuss religion and, specifically, the role of Jesus (or some other empowering figure) as a positive introject for the social phobic. It should also be noted that "relinquishing" of the phobia is highly unlikely. An appropriate therapeutic goal is significant diminishment of the phobia's control over the patient's life and the realization of greater autonomy and decision making.

As noted, Meissner et al. do not discuss social phobia. They confine their discussion to specific phobia and agoraphobia. Zerbe (1994), however, centers explicitly on social phobia and brings a psychoanalytic perspective to it. She criticizes contemporary psychoanalysis for its current neglect of the phobias—social phobia in particular—citing Gabbard and Heinz Kohut as noteworthy exceptions. While Freud's case of Little Hans (a specific phobia) is the best known of his own studies of phobia, Zerbe points out that the case of Emma, "Frau Emmy von N." (actually Baroness Fanny Moser), reported in Breuer and Freud (1955), would be viewed today as social phobia. While Freud treated Emmy as suffering from hysteria, she notes that Emmy's history fulfills many of the *DSM-IV* criteria for social phobia. Emmy alluded, for example, to her "dread of strangers, and of people in general." Observing that Freud could only help Emmy when he abandoned his customary theories and began to listen to her, Zerbe suggests that the psychoanalyst needs especially to "hear" the socially phobic patient. When one does so, she will likely be surprised "by how often human encounters with shame, trauma, and loss play major roles in the etiology of social phobia" (A10).

Like Gabbard, Zerbe recognizes the role of shame as an underlying dynamic in social phobia. She notes that the socially phobic patient who struggles with underlying shame is terrified that others will come to know who he really is and that he will be found sorely lacking. By avoiding the feared performance situations in which he might fail, he also avoids taking risks and experiencing the potential ridicule and frustration that might occur should he fail. In contrast, persons more at peace with their own uniqueness realize that success and failure are part of everyday life. Such individuals have developed "a stable self-image, unperturbed by overwhelming narcissism, greed, hostility, selfishness, competition, and envy" (A11). They can discharge appropriate aggression and competition into culturally sanctioned social activities such as sports. They can also laugh at themselves. The individual who struggles with shame is a different story. To protect herself from even greater vulnerability and exposure, she avoids the situations she most fears by "hiding her light under a bushel." Her behavior reveals a deep lack of trust in others to accept her for her uniqueness, assets and liabilities alike. As a result, a wide array of gratifying and challenging experiences are never undertaken. Fear of humiliation hinders her from truly testing her wings, and prohibits her from knowing the limits of her range.

Zerbe also recognizes that aggression may be an aspect of social phobia, and notes that it is sometimes disguised under the cover of shame, which the patient views as more acceptable. She cites in this connection Miller's (1985) observation that one may emphasize the foolish rather than the aggressive aspect of one's actions because it is less threatening to see one's self as humiliated than as hostile.

Zerbe provides a case illustration of a socially phobic woman who sought therapy because she was chronically unhappy. She was unable to achieve the professional success she desired and was very unfulfilled in her personal relationships. As therapy continued, the phobic features of her problem became more evident. Ostensibly, the central dynamic in the development of her social phobia was her relationship with her father, a scholarly engineer, who had scolded her as a child for any grade less than an A, especially in math. When she began to demonstrate essay and poetry writing abilities to the point of winning some literary contests, he needled her for her lack of interest in math and in girls' athletics. He also demeaned her for her inability to beat him at pinochle and bridge. From her perspective, she was faced with an unsolvable dilemma. If she tried to win her father's approval by academic achievement based on her natural abilities, he rejected her. Unable and unwilling to fulfill his other dreams and aspirations for her, she retreated from the anger she felt out of fear of his retaliation. She also felt that her brother was unavailable and unable to give her comfort.

As an adult, conflicts about performances extended well beyond her family. She remained as quiet as she could, never sharing her "secret" poetry with anyone until well into her third year of psychoanalysis. In fact, it was when she declined a request to read some of her poems on accepting a national writing award that the extent of her social phobia became apparent. When this occurred, she and her therapist (Zerbe) realized that her fear of performance in this situation dovetailed with worries about other social situations. For example, dating provoked enormous anxiety. While she never turned to alcohol to self-medicate, became seriously depressed, or exhibited suicidal ideations, her social phobia substantially interfered with her professional and social interactions. She was convinced that she could never "measure up" to the demands of other people, whether a boss, an audience, or a mate.

Zerbe examines this case from the perspective of Kohut's self-psychology (1971, 1977, 1984). She focuses on the patient's relationship to her mother, noting that the woman's need as a child to be mirrored and valued for her talents and for her own self were not met by either parent. Lacking affirmation, she began to fragment, which lead to a host of psychiatric symptomatology. Experiences that would normally produce joy when met with delight and approval by her parents were conspicuous by their absence. Instead, as a child she was incessantly and mercilessly assailed. She became "understandably alarmed at even the thought of allowing her gifts to come out from behind the shadows. Haughtily criticized by the parental selfobject, she avoided public appearance and certain performance situations...By the apprehensive, cowering responses of the maternal selfobject (her mother had never challenged her father's overbearing manner), she became overwhelmed and panicky when exposed to the feared social situation" (A14). Thus, her paternal selfobject was responsible for one aspect of her phobic condition (her avoidance behavior) while her maternal selfobject accounted for the other (her highly anxious reaction in social situations that she chose *not* to avoid).

Zerbe believes that the more fundamental of these parental selfobjects (or introjects) was the maternal one. In her judgment the woman's personal insecurity stemmed from her mother's acceptance of her father's demeaning outbursts with a cowering demeanor and self-sacrificial attitude: "Without the experience of a calming mother as a selfobject who would nurture self-soothing capacities to allay the spread of anxiety, she lacked the capacity to soothe herself" (A14). The basic problem in all phobias, according to Kohut, is that the individual has a "structural deficit," in this case, a "deficiency in calming structures" (Kohut 1984, 30). Thus, from the perspective of psychoanalytic self-psychology, her unsolvable dilemma with her father as a result of her desire for his approval versus her unwillingness to fulfill his aspirations for her was the surface of a deeper, underlying problem, namely that her mother failed to provide the "calming structure" that she needed. Without it, she was greatly in danger of self-loss, even self-fragmentation. While agoraphobia, with its panicky feeling that one is in danger of losing control or falling apart, is symptomatically similar to this self-fragmentation, Kohut contends that the danger of self-fragmentation is the underlying dynamic of all phobias. This is because they all have at their core an uncontrollable anxiety, attributable to the fact that the child lacks a "calming structure" capable of forestalling and containing her anxieties (Kohut 1984, 30–31).

This psychoanalytic self-psychology perspective is supported by the fact that the patient's social phobia appeared following her mother's death. She confided to Zerbe that she grew up worrying about when her mother's next "breakdown" would occur. She felt she had to walk on tiptoe so as not to threaten her mother's fragile equilibrium, and she was both compliant with and subservient to her mother's needs. Beneath her compliance and subservience, however, she had hostile, even hateful emotions toward her mother, for which she felt guilty. This guilt became unbearable after her mother's death, an event that represented her own "failure" ultimately to protect her mother.

These hostile emotions were, in turn, projected onto the therapist. In Zerbe's view, this projection brings attention to the need for the therapist to be empathic toward her socially phobic patient, because the therapist needs to help her develop, through the therapeutic relationship, the "self-structure" that should have been developed in early childhood. Such empathy should be coupled with a firm resistance to the patient's "defensive strategies of displacement, projection, and avoidance, the very defense mechanisms that most commonly signify phobic neurosis" (A17). Zerbe acknowledges that when the patient projected her hostile feelings toward her mother onto her, she felt herself being drawn into "a temporary state of social phobia" herself. Fear of humiliation temporarily caused her to hesitate "to speak my mind to [the patient's] devaluating, vigilant, angry internalized maternal image" (A13).

Conclusion

In this and the two preceding chapters, we have reviewed the most prominent psychological (as opposed to pharmacological) treatment approaches to social phobia. There are various other psychological approaches to the treatment of social phobics that were not discussed, such as the use of imaginal desensitization (exposing phobics to pictures of the feared situation) and hypnosis (Baker and Boaz 1983; Lamb 1985;

Mott 1986). Omission of these other methods seemed justified, however, because they are more commonly used with specific phobias. Furthermore, their techniques are as inaccessible to the general reader (for whom this book is intended) as are the pharmacological methods that I have also omitted.

One of the more striking developments in the treatment of social phobics is the increasing use of systematically eclectic approaches. As Zerbe points out, therapists are discovering that they may learn much more about the disorder if they refuse "to stay bound and beholden to any *one* theory or treatment method" (A17). An obvious rationale for systematic eclecticism is that no single treatment method has proven to be overwhelmingly effective with social phobia. This is partly due to the fact that there are different types of social phobia (or different "situational domains"). Another reason is that social phobia is a commentary on the whole of human social life. Social phobics are highly sensitized to the downside of social interaction while harboring high, even utopian, views of what human social interaction *could* be. In this sense, social phobia is more than a personal pathology. Social phobia is also an implicit critique of human social life as we know it, especially of its dominance/submissiveness manifestations. Human social interaction is enormously complex. As a perspective on human social interaction, social phobia is also complex. Therefore, reliance on a single treatment method for social phobia gives too much weight to one conception (or misconception) of human social interaction.

If we opt for a systematic eclecticism, however, we should recognize that not all of these treatment methods are easily or even potentially reconcilable to one another. For example, the psychoanalytic position that social phobia reflects an internal conflict and that the external situation is a symbolic representation of this internal conflict is not easily reconciled with a cognitive-behavioral approach that seeks to change the client's distorted conception of external situations. Both agree that the patient is mistaken in his perception of the external situation. For cognitive therapists, however, the fact that he has a distorted view of the social situation matters a great deal, whereas, for the psychoanalyst, it seems not to matter very much. Instead, what matters to the psychoanalyst is the internalization of early childhood interpersonal experiences, mainly involving parents. As the psychoanalytic cases presented in this chapter indicate, the psychoanalyst devotes much more attention to the patient's projections of internal conflicts onto the external world (or the "social world" of the patient-therapist relationship) than to exploration of the social situations in which phobic reactions are aroused.

On the other hand, to the extent that we *can* respond affirmatively to Zerbe's plea that we not become "bound and beholden" to any single treatment approach, we may be able to discern unexpected compatibilities between seemingly irreconcilable orientations because we are free to operate somewhat more pragmatically than those who are committed to a single treatment approach. We should also be mindful of the fact, noted by several authors discussed in these three chapters, that success in the treatment of social phobics is often attributable to factors of which the therapist is unaware. Cognitive-behavioral therapists, for example, have emphasized the need to question whether exposure to the feared social situation accounts for a client's improvement or whether other factors were more significant. While this argument is often made to criticize a competing therapeutic method, it may also support the more positive, albeit humbling, view that we do not really know all the factors that are involved in therapeutic improvements, any more than we know all the factors that are involved in the pathology's formation and persistence over time. What we *do* know is that social phobia is a difficult problem to diagnose and to treat. We therefore need to be wary of any treatment approach that claims quick and easy cures for social phobia. If it is possible, as Zerbe puts it, for social phobics' lives to become "more bearable," this is no small achievement and is to be celebrated, however it comes about.

CHAPTER 7

Cultural Dimensions
of
Social Phobia

A weakness of the research and therapeutic literature on social phobia is that it does not give much attention to cultural influences, especially on how social phobics experience and interpret their disability. While social phobia is a universal phenomenon with a long and complex evolutionary history, how it is viewed and interpreted depends in part on the cultural value (or disvalue) placed on it. In turn, these cultural views and interpretations may determine the degree of suffering that the social phobic experiences and may even determine whether a given individual "qualifies" for the clinical diagnosis of social phobia.

To address these cultural issues, I will focus on Okano's (1994) transcultural analysis of social phobia as experienced in contemporary Japan and the United States. By focusing on only these two sociocultural contexts, the variety of ways in which social phobia has been interpreted and evaluated historically and throughout the world will necessarily be shortchanged. By treating these two sociocultural settings in greater depth, however, we gain an idea of how deeply the very experience of social phobia is influenced by cultural understandings and thus how profoundly they affect the lives of those who, by innate temperament, are at risk to develop into social phobics later in life. This particular comparison also enables us to explore the complexities of the dynamic interaction of shame and guilt themes in the cultural interpretation of social phobia and especially to take exception to the simplistic notion that Asian societies are "shame-based" while Western societies are "guilt-based."

Okano's analysis of social phobia in Japan and the United States focuses on the role of shame in social phobia. His major objective is to offer a broad and relativistic view of shame by bringing a transcultural perspective to bear on social phobia. His perspective derives from his personal experience as a practicing psychiatrist in both cultures. In his view, the literatures on shame produced by the psychiatric communities of the two countries are "culture-bound," but their viewpoints are complementary, revealing each other's blind spots. He offers his own alternative view which encompasses both perspectives.

While emphasizing the role of culture in shaping the meanings of shame, he emphasizes that his own transcultural approach to shame does not eliminate the significance of innate temperament, "which may determine one's shame-proneness and propensity to social phobia." However, "It is the meaning people attach to the experience of shame that is dependent on the socio-cultural context" (324).

Beginning with Japan, he notes that for Japanese psychiatrists, shame and shyness play an important role in the pathogenesis of several mental disorders, including social phobia, paranoia, and depression. In general, Japanese psychiatrists appear to assume that the culturally-encouraged show of shame-proneness is enough to explain the reported high prevalence of social phobia in Japan. These psychiatrists also argue that social phobia has a much higher prevalence in Japan than in the Western world. Okano, however, points to the difficulty of determining whether this is in fact the case, mainly because there is a lack of comparative epidemiological data on social phobia in the two countries. A study of psychiatric outpatients in a Japanese mental hospital indicated that 2.5 percent had a primary diagnosis of social phobia. While this is not a powerful demonstration of a high prevalence of social phobia in Japan, it is widely believed that there is a large "subclinical" population of socially phobic persons in Japan. One study showed that nearly one-third of the new students in a Japanese university indicated that they flushed easily or were overly aware of the gaze of others. Another report indicated that about 50 percent of the students in another university had a "tendency" toward social phobia.

Thus, the question is whether there is an extensive "subclinical" or "subthreshold" incidence of social phobia in Japan. Japanese psychiatrists generally agree that there is. Whether it is much larger than the subclinical population in the United States is impossible to determine on the basis of existing data. In any case, Okano believes that this question cannot be answered without taking into account the different ways in which social phobia manifests itself in the two cultures. He agrees with the Japanese psychiatric community that the high prevalence of

subclinical social phobia symptoms in Japan compared with Western society could be related to "the socially promoted show of shame among Japanese people" (327). He suggests that Japanese society may well be a "pseudo-sociophobic" culture because so many cultural phenomena that are considered proper in Japanese society are phenomenologically similar to subclinical forms of sociophobic symptoms. What Japanese culture promotes is not the feeling of shame itself but the external manifestations of the feeling of shame in sociophobic-like symptoms. In other words, what is promoted is not shame as such but the "sense of shame," or awareness and sensitivity to the actual experience of shame.

In support of this view, Okano cites typical examples of this culturally-promoted show of shame. Staring at other people, for example, especially one's elders or superiors, is considered impolite. Verbal assertiveness and making one's opinion too clear and distinct in public is also regarded as improper. It is unwise to show off one's competence and competitiveness to others and it is regarded as taboo not to be in touch with one's feelings of shame. In the Japanese language, a person who does not understand shame is equivalent to a "thick-skinned" and "insensitive" person who is practically unfit for society. Thus, to be accepted in society, individuals are required to "fake" sociophobic-like manifestations. It seems reasonable therefore to assume that a certain number of Japan's populace will develop "real" symptoms of social phobia, such as a genuine fear of eye-to-eye confrontation and of oral communication that centers around assertiveness. Under these conditions, it may be difficult to determine who is in fact socially phobic and who is simply acting in a socially-approved manner.

This raises the question of what social purposes are served by a culturally-approved use of external manifestations of the feeling of shame in sociophobic-like symptoms? In Okano's view, their most obvious function is to reduce the society's envy-driven competitiveness: "Every show of an individual's strength and assertiveness is carefully modified or camouflaged in this society so that an individual is better accepted. Verbal assertiveness and staring straight into another's face are discouraged because they are regarded as a provocative, defiant show of one's own power and strength" (327). In contrast, one's bashful and overpowered looks, lack of verbal assertiveness, and avoidance of gaze, all of which mimic the appearance of "true" sociophobic symptoms, demonstrate one's weakness, limitations, and inadequacy. This reduces the potential for arousing jealousy and feelings of competitiveness in others. Thus, for the Japanese, the show of shame can be actively used to reduce friction in social relationships.

Okano attributes this exhibition of shame to a belief generally shared by Japanese people that a person's importance, power, or value should only be implied or suggested, never openly revealed. This belief implies that what is hidden is powerful and what is manifest has already lost its power or value. This belief has a long history in Japanese culture. For example, a fifteenth-century manual on the art of flower arranging counsels that "what is concealed is the flower. What is not concealed cannot be the flower." Thus, because an essence must be concealed to be truly essential, true strength should be hidden by those who have it unless it reveals itself naturally. The point is not that one should not be strong and capable, but that one should not reveal these traits spontaneously, for such restraint proves the individual's *real* strength and ability. This means that "a well-adapted sociophobic-like person" should have an inner strength and confidence that makes him "immune to the culturally promoted submissive and self-defeating attitude, which otherwise would hurt the person's pride and narcissistic self-image" (328–329).

Okano cites two psychoanalytic studies by Kitayama (1985, 1987) in support of his argument that strength is associated with that which is hidden. In one study (1985), Kitayama focused on the prevalent theme in Japanese folklore of the taboo against looking. In many folktales, the hero's violation of this prohibition, usually by looking at his attractive lover's nakedness, has a disastrous outcome. Instead of a beautiful woman, the hero sees an animal that is an ugly mixture of split images, the "good" and "bad" mother. Even though this taboo is expected to be violated (in contrast to the incest taboo, which is never violated), the abundance of this type of folklore in Japan indicates the belief that revelation will spoil one's positive values. It also implies that there is a shameful side (dark, ugly, etc.) even to the most beautiful and attractive person. The decision to look is therefore to invite disillusionment.

In the second study, Kitayama (1987) pointed out that the Japanese language is generally used loosely and is grammatically ill-structured. He believes this serves the tendency of the Japanese to communicate ideas while leaving them unspoken. Thus, language itself manifests the socially approved cultural value of hiding in order to preserve values and to contain or withhold individual prerogatives. Kitayama suggests a possible relationship between the ambiguity of the Japanese language and the (apparently) high prevalence of social phobia. As Okana explains, Kitayama's idea of a "morbid fear of ambiguity" in Japanese society refers to "the paranoid fear of being misunderstood by others because of their secretive and ambiguous mode of speech, which is inherent in the sentence structure of Japanese language" (329).

Okano concludes that Japanese society "promotes a sociophobic-like attitude, with humility and self-deprecating gestures in social relationships and with a resultant proliferation of shame-prone, avoidant, and sensitive demeanor similar to social phobia" (329). This "feigned" socially phobic attitude has at least two adaptive functions. It inhibits the envy and competiveness that a show of one's capacity and strength would elicit in others, and it protects one's strength—and vulnerability—by keeping them invisible to others as well as to oneself, so that they remain unchallenged and unharmed by others. While it serves these adaptive functions, however, Okano believes that it may have another unintended function. This is that "the abundance of pseudo-sociopathic attitudes among the Japanese tends to facilitate the occurrence of true sociophobic symptoms, which are maladaptive and dysfunctional" (329). A related problem is that persons who are genuinely sociophobic, perhaps by virtue of an innate shyness, may not be distinguishable from those who are not. That they appear to be no different from others may paradoxically make them feel even more isolated.

Turning to American society, Okano notes that, in striking contrast to Japanese society, there are few customs or moral codes that promote self-effacing, inhibited, and avoidant attitudes toward others. It is not, for example, considered impolite to gaze at other people. Rather, avoiding eye contact is often interpreted as a show of vulnerability, insecurity, even dishonesty or deviousness. American society also actively promotes verbal assertiveness and making one's opinion known as clearly and distinctly as possible. Furthermore, American society values the open show of competitiveness. Showing one's ability and power in a most visible and tangible manner through self-promotional behavior seems to be the "royal road to success." Okano cites Christopher Lasch's argument (1979) that this tendency has become even more pervasive in recent decades, as individuals are devoted "to superficial images and personal advancement." Citing Lasch's contention that narcissism appears to represent the best way of coping with the tensions and anxieties of modern life, he concludes that the United States is a "narcissistic society," one that "constantly pressures people to manifest their strengths and abilities in the most overt and visible way, if they want to thrive socially" (330).

The direct opposite of the pseudo-sociophobic society, this narcissistic quality of American social life offers a strong protection against vulnerability to feelings of shame and inferiority. Narcissistic strivings are a show of active avoidance of—even a counterphobic attitude toward—acknowledging one's experiences of shame. In effect, the narcissistic society dictates that the winners will be those who successfully hide their vulnerability to shame and their sense of inferiority behind their narcissistic, grandiose facade. On the other hand, American society believes more easily than Japanese society in what is visible and obvious and takes a very negative view of secrecy and hiding. If what is hidden needs to be revealed, this accounts in part for the general trend toward openly discussing the shameful features of American life (such as marital violence, incest, sexual abuse) that lie behind its grandiose facade of achievement and power. This also means, however, that shame, in the sense of hiding, inhibition, and avoidance, is considered a negative personal trait because it reflects an inherent secretive nature. Thus, real shame, the shame that is so deeply and truly felt that it resists all social pressures for exposure, is considered both psychologically unhealthy and morally suspect.

This means that in America the shame that is endemic to social phobia is considered to have little social value. Therefore, social phobia itself is problematic, both psychologically and morally. The result may be either an underdiagnosis of social phobia or a belated recognition of its true prevalence. In support of this view, Okano notes that much of the current American psychiatric literature on shame reflects the "central dogma" that the feeling of shame is not a healthy emotional experience, and the goal of treatment should therefore be to decrease or eliminate it altogether. Only a minority of authors view shame as a positive emotion, either as an expression of modesty or discretion or as a check against the "shamelessness" of a narcissistic society in which no secrets are kept, nothing is held in confidence, and no self-display, however extravagant or uninhibited, is proscribed.

Based on his comparative analysis of the two societies, Okano offers his own perspective, one that encompasses both sociocultural worldviews. In formulating his own point of view, he accepts as a given that vulnerability to shame is universal and is therefore the experience of members of both societies. Given this vulnerability to shame, there are a significant number of social phobics in both societies, that is, persons whose vulnerability to shame is much more pronounced, distressing, or anxiety-arousing than it is for those who are better able to manage their vulnerability (partly because of the very cultural processes identified: pseudo-shame in Japan and narcissism in the United States). Okano's starting point for his alternative perspective is the fact that the two societies take either a positive or a negative view of that which is hidden. In his view, the act of hiding is itself neither good or bad, and it would not cause problems unless an individual were no longer aware of what she is hiding and for what purpose: "In other words, the act of hiding becomes pathological when it involves hiding from oneself" (335).

In psychoanalytic terms, the theory of repression makes a similar argument. Like that which is hidden, repressed wishes and impulses are not necessarily pathological. They become pathological when they cannot be brought to awareness. Therefore, the issue is whether a society can view that which is hidden from the perspective, or principle, of flexibility. In Okano's view, Japan and the United States are two societies that are largely incapable of employing the principle of flexibility. Instead, they represent the two extremes in terms of how that which is hidden is valued. He cites Freud's view in *The Ego and the Id* (1961) that guilt causes problems when it is either totally repressed (in hysteria) or over-strongly conscious (in obsessional neurosis and melancholia). In these pathologies, there seems to be no middle ground. Thus, in Freud's view, guilt will not become pathological if the individual (via the ego) can exercise some "free rein" in determining whether the guilt is conscious or unconscious. This is the only way that a person can be at peace with guilt-provoking thoughts and wishes: "Guilt should be neither totally repressed nor constantly under the scrutiny of consciousness; instead, it should be able to move back and forth from unconscious to conscious, depending on the circumstances" (335). Furthermore, "this pendulum-like flexibility and mobility should occur rather naturally, because any guilt-provoking wish has a reason to be both repressed (because of its potentially unethical and sinful nature) and in full awareness (because the person cannot always afford to use mental energy to repress it)" (335). What causes psychopathology is the rigidity of the wish's relationship to consciousness and unconsciousness alike.

Okano suggests that this same principle of flexibility versus rigidity may be applied to the experience of shame. From this viewpoint, neither Japanese nor American cultural attitudes are sufficiently concerned about the flexibility in what is hidden: "The Japanese tend to glorify and attach too much value to what is hidden, whereas Americans in general tend to devalue and minimize what is hidden and instead try to disclose it" (335). Ideally, in Japan, the cultivation of secrets produces self-empowerment. For historical or social reasons, however, the Japanese have not been able to take full advantage of the possibilities that are inherent in their cultural habit of keeping things hidden. Instead of it being viewed as the source of an empowered self, the opposite has occurred, as the secrecy tends to favor self-repression and self-inhibition. Okano believes that if the Japanese could develop greater flexibility with regard to the disclosure of things hidden, they would feel that they are in control of the act of hiding, fully in charge of deciding when and what to disclose or not to disclose.

By the same token, Americans could profit from a more flexible attitude toward the positive and empowering uses of secrecy and hiding. If Americans would no longer attach an exclusively positive value to what is manifest and visible, with a corresponding neglect of the value of secretiveness, they would feel less need to resort to their narcissistic strivings and would more readily admit their painful vulnerability to shame and a sense of inferiority. They would then believe that they could still be valuable even if they do not visibly appear to be so. This need not become the superficial self-disclosiveness to which Americans are prone. Instead, it would manifest the same exercise of judgment over what is disclosed or not disclosed that Okano recommends to the Japanese. The point is that it becomes a matter of personal autonomy and decision.

Okano does not develop the implications for social phobia of his more flexible approach to what is hidden. We can readily discern, however, what it may mean for social phobia. For example, if social phobics operate on the assumption that they should try to "expose" themselves to all of the social situations that cause them to become anxious and fearful, Okano's flexibility principle suggests instead that they should allow themselves to assume personal control over the "act of hiding" (or "avoidance"). This means being fully in charge of deciding when and where they will "expose" themselves to anxiety-arousing social situations. The therapeutic goal is not "full exposure," but the exercise of autonomy and personal decision-making. This, in turn, will lead to greater self-empowerment.

While this conclusion might appear to conflict with much of the therapeutic literature on social phobia, it is supported by several of the theories we have reviewed. For example, the social skills training approach now places great emphasis on "self-management skills." While such skills are usually employed in behalf of greater social involvement, they *could* just as well be used to enable a socially-phobic person to be in greater control of the event of exposure, placing her in the position of deciding when and where to expose herself to the social situations that she normally fears. The reframing method of the cognitive-behavioral therapists makes this point even more explicitly. It involves assuring clients that they have every right *not* to socialize. The therapist reframes the problematic behavior as legitimate choices and suggests that these behaviors should be practiced and explored in that spirit. Also, while the symptom prescription method in cognitive-behavioral therapy does not ordinarily extend to avoidance of the social situation altogether, there is no reason why this extension might not also be made: "If you avoid the situation that causes you to feel anxious, do so with a full sense of the legitimacy of your personal decision to avoid it." After all, the same "right to avoid" is regularly accorded persons who have specific phobias (fear of certain animals, heights, noises, etc.).

The fact that the right to avoid stressful social situations has not been a prominent feature of social phobia treatment in the United States reflects American cultural values regarding exposure of that which is hidden. The fact that the "exposure method" was the first to be applied to social phobia, and that it continues to be used alongside other methods, indicates the degree to which these cultural values have influenced social phobia treatment. Okano's argument in favor of flexibility suggests that the decision to expose or not expose oneself to a stressful situation is an individual matter, and that whatever the decision happens to be, it warrants our respect and approval.

This affirmation of the individual's right to avoid certain stressful situations is precisely where a psychology of guilt may have particular relevance to social phobia. Social phobics feel personal shame for being unable to attend dreaded social gatherings or for turning down requests to perform in public. They also feel guilty, however, for failing in these situations to meet or fulfill the expectations that others have of them. In fact, this is where social phobics often feel most vulnerable, for they are greatly concerned that, in avoiding a dreaded situation, they have placed their own needs above those who have invited or requested their presence or performance. Social phobics need to be reassured and to reassure themselves that they have committed no crime nor violated any moral injunction by exercising their right to avoid a stressful situation. A "subthreshold social phobic" of my personal acquaintance once told me that she struggled with her anxieties about participating in a woman's social club but usually attended because she felt guilty if she did not attend. Within a year, however, the club disbanded because its founder and leader decided to apply her energies toward forming another group, one to which the socially phobic woman was never invited.

To be sure, social phobics need to consider to what extent they are using their phobia to justify or rationalize social indolence. For the vast majority of social phobics, however, this is not the basis for their avoidance habits. As noted earlier in our review of psychoanalytic treatment theories, social phobics may, in fact, have begun to avoid social situations in childhood because they were made to feel guilty over their desire to be the center of attention. If so, this suggests that social phobics are not reclusive or isolative by nature, but are unable to act on their affiliative predispositions in certain social situations. Many seek therapy because they would dearly love to be able to perform in public settings, and they hope that through therapy they will be able to overcome their inhibitions.

In short, Okano's principle of flexibility applies to all features of social phobia, inhibition but also avoidance. It also relates to every sub-type or social domain of social phobia identified by Holt et al. (1992): formal interaction, informal interaction, assertiveness, and observation by others. By presenting this principle in the context of an analysis of the different meanings that cultures assign to shame, Okano relativizes the views of a given society toward social phobia and those that social phobics in these societies may have of themselves. Such relativizing supports cognitive theorists' view that "unconditional beliefs about the self" typically held by social phobics are excessively and inappropriately negative. By showing that views of inhibited behavior are culturally relative, Okano invites a more tolerant view of socially phobic persons and a less self-condemnatory attitude by social phobics themselves. The behavior of the American social phobic is the very behavior that Japanese society has sought to cultivate, while the self-promotional behavior that America highly values is considered rude and offensive in Japanese society. One society's pathology is another's society's cultural ideal.

This does not mean that social phobia is not a debilitating condition or that it does not have its personal costs. Real social phobics in both societies do find it debilitating, though the ways in which they find it so, and the precise nature of the costs, vary. For the social phobic in Japan, the greatest cost may be that one's social phobia remains hidden, even perhaps from oneself, because it does not differ overtly from "pseudo" sociophobic-like behaviors. For the social phobic in America, the greater costs may be in areas of social success (such as job promotion or marital prospects) because the social phobic is at a distinct social disadvantage in comparison with persons who are able to participate less anxiously in the areas of social interaction most valued by the society.

That social phobia is inherently distressing because it involves feelings of anxiety and fear is not to be denied or discounted. The fact that its social meanings are culturally determined means, however, that one's inherent vulnerability is either exacerbated or alleviated by the cultural meanings attached to social phobic behavior. It also means that the form of social phobia that emerges in a given cultural context is influenced by these meanings. In the United States, social phobics are conspicuous by their difference from the cultural norm of self-promotion, self-assertiveness, vaulting self-confidence, and open competiveness. In Japan, social phobics are an extension of the cultural norm, persons who experience as real and true for them what the others experience as a sociocultural fiction.

On the other hand, the very oppositeness of social phobia in the United States may disguise the fact that social phobics are products of their culture and therefore may share many of its narcissistic values. If they do not manifest personal characteristics of self-promotion and the like, this does not necessarily mean that they do not have the desire to be like the others. It may, in fact, mean that they go about being self-promotional in less overt ways, thus further inviting the social condemnation—and perhaps the self-condemnation—that they are secretive, that is, unwilling or unable to be up front concerning these cultural characteristics and traits. As the psychoanalytic view of social phobia would suggest that they want to be the center of attention (at least unconsciously), they have a deep sense of being in competition with rivals to be noticed and acclaimed, and they may experience themselves as fraudulent and deceptive because they cannot be up front about these desires and aspirations.

In this sense, social phobics are no more the paragons of virtue than those who are openly narcissistic. Indeed, their tendency to engage in self-scrutiny causes them to see things about themselves that members of the dominant group do not or cannot see about *themselves*. In this sense, they confirm the belief of the Japanese folklore tradition that the violation of the taboo against observing may result in disillusionment. The taboo that is violated in this case, however, is not gazing at another but at one's inner self. In gazing at the inner self, seeing the self in the harsh and unforgiving glare of reality, the social phobic experiences self-disillusionment, seeing himself all too clearly, which is what feeling shame is fundamentally about. Thus, for the social phobic, his very own self is what he experiences as vulnerable and, more distressingly, as seriously flawed. If social phobics therefore expect that they will be subject to the negative judgments of others, this is because they already view themselves rather negatively. What they desperately need—and both envy and disparage in their dominant counterparts—is the capacity to view themselves with a substantial degree of creative illusion. Like Freud's obsessive/compulsives and melancholics, the social phobic seems to need to bring everything about himself to consciousness, something that the self-promotional narcissist would never do.

We may draw an analogy here between social phobics and depressives. Recent research on depressives has found that depressed persons actually have more accurate perceptions of the world and of themselves than nondepressives do. Fisher and Fisher, the authors who report this finding, are therefore concerned to make a case for "the self-protective value of illusion" (1993, 10). Like depressives, the social phobic's relentless self-scrutiny leaves her vulnerable to the same difficulty, to what the authors call "the discomfort of realism" (4). In effect, the social phobic knows *too much* about herself and is under none of the illusions that enable those who are dominant by nature to assume positions of power, leadership, and local and national celebrity.

In noting the self-protective (as well as the self-serving) value of illusion, we are verging on the issues that will concern us in the next chapter. Religion may be viewed as the source of illusions (Pruyser 1983) that, unlike those produced by alcohol and other self-medications, have genuine and lasting power to alleviate the anxieties of social phobics to the point where these become self-manageable.

Conclusion

Okano's cultural approach to social phobia suggests that there is something very concrete and pragmatic that social phobics may do to reduce their fears and anxieties concerning the various "situational domains" to which they are vulnerable. This is that social phobics (both clinical and subthreshold) may adopt a more *flexible* view toward their involvement in feared social situations, viewing each involvement as a matter of personal choice. Contrary to the "exposure" treatment method, which advocates a graduated exposure to the feared situation until anxiety is permanently extinguished, the principle of flexibility operates on a self-conscious decision-making basis. "I will attend the Williams' party ('They are nice, unassuming people') but forego the Johnson's party ('They're too showy')." "I will make the report in Professor Thomson's course ('He seems easygoing and the class is small') but I will ask Professor Klein ('He scares me, and the other students know a lot more than I do about the subject') if I may be relieved of the report assignment and write an extra paper instead." "I will return the dress myself ('The salespersons at Penney's never ask why I'm returning something and are also so cheerful about it') but I will ask my husband to return the shoes ('I should never have shopped at Neiman-Marcus in the first place')." "I will return Sarah Smith's call ('She sounded nervous on the phone') but I'll not return Lois Jones's call ('She's always so officious and self-important')." "I will speak to my supervisor about taking an extra day off, but I'll let someone else tell him that Frank is hurting office morale."

In other words, the social phobic begins to make finer discriminations between feared situations and exercises personal control over ones she is prepared to approach and ones she will continue to avoid. In making these discriminations, she does not then chastise herself for choosing to avoid certain situations, for the goal is not to become perfectly at ease in every social situation that might arise, but to become more at ease in those in which she *does* choose to participate. The goal is not the elimination of all social anxiety but the exercise of self-management in the very decision whether or not to become involved. In effect, she draws on insights from the social skills treatment method, which emphasizes self-management as opposed to automatic deference to the expectations of others; the self-efficacy approach, which emphasizes doing those things that she believes she is capable of doing; and reframing theory, which emphasizes that she has a perfect right *not* to participate in a social situation (even in her occupational life) in which she feels uncomfortable. Avoidance is not a sign of moral or psychological weakness.

Admittedly, I have taken the principle of flexibility in a direction that Okano does not explicitly endorse. This is consistent, however, with his view that the problem with Japanese and American cultures is their excessively rigid perspectives on shame, which, in turn, result in attitudes toward social phobic behavior that are also excessively rigid. Also, in the above illustrations, I have viewed the dominance/submissiveness dynamics of social situations as a key consideration in the decision-making process. If the social phobic anticipates that a social situation will place him in a very uncomfortable position regarding this dynamic, this should constitute a warning that exposure to the situation will not have its intended effect of reducing his anxiety and contributing to the eventual diminishment of his fears. Instead, it will predictably have the very opposite effect. Not indiscriminate exposure, but discriminating decision making, is the approach that the principle of flexibility invites us to endorse and adopt. In this way, one goes a long way toward reducing the guilt that magnifies social phobia's capacity to induce anxiety.

CHAPTER 8

Religious Alleviations
for Social Phobia

The issue that I want to address in this chapter is whether religion has something of value to offer social phobics. In chapter 2, the role of religion both in precipitating and in alleviating the fear associated with social phobia was briefly discussed. In this chapter, I want to explore in greater depth the question of whether religion may alleviate the fear associated with social phobia and, if so, in what ways? My reason for asking whether religion may be helpful in this regard is that social phobia has its basis in an *excessive* fear of external threat. As we have seen, the psychoanalytic tradition attributes its excessiveness to the fact that the fears result from internal conflicts that have been projected onto the external situation. If this argument has merit, we may appropriately ask whether religion may help to alleviate these internal conflicts. Following the psychoanalytic argument that a positive introject or self-object (such as a therapist) can help to overcome the damage that has been done by negative introjects or selfobjects (such as parents), we may ask whether and in what ways religion might be the source of positive selfobjects whose function is to alleviate the anxieties associated with social phobia.

To address this question, I will first turn to William James, author of *The Varieties of Religious Experience* (1982; originally published in 1902). James took great interest in the psychological study of phobias. This was in part because he had personal experiences that were phobic in nature. These experiences gave him an acute sensitivity to the pain that phobias may cause. They were also instrumental in his decision to study what religious writers had to say about the experience of fear. That he wrote *The Varieties* relatively late in life (age sixty) suggests that his personal interest in religion was not born of youthful enthusiasm.

Instead, it reflected the religious longings of an older man who was deeply acquainted with fears that had proven remarkably persistent throughout his life in spite of the fact that, as a psychologist, he had considerable intellectual knowledge about them.

In addition to drawing on James, I will also use Heinz Kohut, the psychoanalytic selfpsychologist introduced in chapter 6, to frame a consideration of Jesus as a spiritual resource in the social phobic's struggle with anxiety. My proposal is that, for persons of Christian background, Jesus may function for the social phobic as an internalized self-object who offers grounds for *not* being anxious and also challenges the dominance/submissiveness system of the social order. In doing so, he empowers the social phobic to participate in the subversion of this system. For readers who identify with other religious traditions, there are comparable figures or personages who may serve—as Jesus does for Christianity—the role of the internalized selfobject. There are other figures in Christianity—such as saints and other exemplary individuals—who may also take on this role for those for whom Jesus is not a plausible self-object. My point is not that only Jesus can function in this manner but that he is illustrative of how a religious personage *may* so function.

William James and the Enveloping Presence of God

James had a lifelong interest in pathological fear, due in part to the fact that he experienced a severe panic attack in his mid-twenties. Describing this experience in *The Varieties of Religious Experience*, he relates that he went into a closet to get a piece of clothing and, without any prior warning, he was overwhelmed with "a horrible fear of my own existence" (1982, 160). As he described the experience, "It was as if something hitherto solid within my breast gave way entirely, and I became a mass of quivering fear" (160). While this experience precipitated a nervous breakdown that lasted several weeks, he believes he would have grown "really insane" had he not clung to certain scripture texts, such as "The eternal God is my refuge" and "Come unto me, all ye who labor and are heavy laden." His description of this panic attack supports Kohut's view that panic involves the feeling that one is in danger of self-fragmentation, a feeling that may be traced, developmentally, to a deficiency in "calming structures" during infancy and early childhood (Kohut 1984, 28–33). Given this personal experience, we should not be surprised that James gave a great deal of attention in *The Varieties* to the relationship between religion and fear, and that he places much more emphasis on how religion may alleviate fear than in how it creates and exacerbates fear.

James's interest in fear was already apparent in his first major book, the two volume *The Principles of Psychology* (1950, originally published in 1890). Here he explored fear as an instinct, illustrating this view with a case of animal phobia. He suggests that animals awaken in a child two opposing impulses, fear and fondling. If, in her first attempts to pat a dog, the child gets snapped at or bitten, so that the impulses of fear are strongly aroused, it may be that for years to come no dog will excite in her the impulse to fondle (1950, 2, 395).

He also considered the issue of fear in his discussion of the emotions. He quotes at length Charles Darwin's account of the physiological symptoms of fear (1950, 2, 446). Later in the same chapter he discusses morbid or pathological fear (460). Two years later, he condensed *The Principles* and published the shorter version under the title *Psychology: The Briefer Course* (1961). In the briefer version, he actually expanded his earlier discussion of fear, using it to illustrate how the emotions work. Here he contends that "fear is a reaction aroused by the same objects that arouse ferocity…We both fear, and wish to kill, anything that may kill me." Because both reactions occur simultaneously, this introduces "an uncertainty into our response to external threat" (275). Further, he notes that fear has "bodily expressions of an extremely energetic kind, and stands, beside lust and anger, as one of the three most exciting emotions of which our nature is susceptible" (275).

On the other hand, he suggests that, in "the progress from brute to man," fear is the emotion that has decreased the most, so much so that in civilized life, it is possible for large numbers of people to pass from cradle to grave without ever having had a pang of fear: "Many of us need an attack of mental disease to teach us the meaning of the word" (275). This decline in experiences of genuine fear explains, in his view, "the possibility of so much blindly optimistic philosophy and religion. The atrocities of life become 'like a tale of little meaning though the words are strong.' We doubt if anything like *us* ever really was within the tiger's jaws, and conclude that the horrors we hear of are but a sort of painted tapestry for the chambers in which we lie so comfortably at peace with ourselves and with the world" (275). He implies in this passage that we need a religion that reflects awareness of fear. This is exactly the task he sets for himself in *The Varieties of Religious Experience*.

In *Psychology: The Briefer Course*, James identifies the major classes of fear. These include loud noises in childhood; strange people and strange animals, especially people and animals who advance toward us in a threatening way; spiders and snakes; solitude (whose etiology can be traced to the infant's inevitable cry of dismay on waking up and finding himself alone); black things, especially dark places, holes, caverns, etc.; high places; fear of the supernatural (ghosts, corpses, etc.); and various pathological fears. Among pathological fears, he cites the case of melancholiacs who, "insane with general anxiety and fear of everything," assume a "statue-like, crouching immobility," reminiscent of the immobility of a threatened beast or a human who hopes the stalker will not perceive its presence. He concludes with a brief mention of agoraphobia and suggests that the agoraphobic's clinging to the sides of a public square or hugging the houses as closely as possible is quite common among rodents, such as squirrels, who "dart across the open as a desperate measure." Thus, agoraphobia may be "the accidental resurrection, through disease," of "an instinct which may in some of our remote ancestors have had a permanent and on the whole a useful part to play" (281).

James's discussion of fear in *Psychology: The Briefer Course* is remarkably similar to Öhman's evolutionary theory of fear, which also focuses on the fear aroused when animals or other humans advance toward us in a threatening way. Among the fears that he identifies, this is the one that falls most naturally under the current classification of social phobia. We may also note that, in his citation of pathological fears, he instances melancholia, describing the melancholiac as assuming a "statue-like, crouching immobility" reminiscent of the immobility of a person or animal who hopes the stalker will not perceive its presence. Melancholia (James's own affliction) is therefore the more pathological form of social phobia because it involves withdrawal from social interaction altogether. Like social phobia, it reflects the impulse to avoid a threatening situation in which one is likely to come out the loser. Here, James seems to be quite aware of the dominance/submissiveness dynamics central to social phobia and even more extreme in melancholia.

James does not discuss the remedies for fear in *Psychology: The Briefer Course*. In *The Varieties of Religious Experience*, however, he is concerned with the efforts that were being made, through the aegis of the mind-cure movement, to alleviate anxiety and fear. Perhaps because he found his own fears remarkably resistant to extinction, the question of whether religion may help to alleviate them acquired great interest for him. This is partly because, immediately prior to writing *The Varieties*, he had suffered another bout of melancholy. This time, he confided to his wife that his customary method of "willing" himself back to health was no longer effective (Lewis 1991, 511). Thus, a decade after *Psychology: The Briefer Course* appeared, he returned in *The Varieties* to the subject of fear.

James's most sustained discussions in *The Varieties* of fear occur in his lectures on "healthy-mindedness" and "the sick soul," the latter of which contains his own experience of panic fear. Whereas more traditional Christian theology has focused on the will and has said that this is "the essential vice" in "the lower part of human nature," the "mind-curers say that the mark of the beast is *fear*," and this "is what gives such an entirely new religious turn to their persuasion" (98). He quotes at length from several mind-cure authors, one who suggests that "fearthought" is the unprofitable element in "forethought," and another who observes that "Man often has fear stamped upon him before his entrance into the outer world; he is reared in fear; all his life is passed in bondage to fear of disease and death, and thus his whole mentality becomes cramped, limited, and depressed, and his body follows its shrunken pattern and specification" (99). This author, Henry Wood, in a book titled *Ideal Suggestion Through Mental Photography*, claims that "nothing but the boundless divine love, exuberance, and vitality, constantly poured in, even though unconsciously to us, could in some degree neutralize such an ocean of morbidity" (99).

James is somewhat critical of the extravagances of the mind-cure authors, especially when they deny the very existence of evil. He is impressed, however, by the "psychological similarity" between the mind-cure movement of his day and the Lutheran and Wesleyan movements of earlier eras. To believers in moralism and works, with their anxious query, "What must I do to be saved?" both Luther and Wesley replied, "You are saved now, if you would but believe it." In James's view, the mind-curers "come with precisely similar words of emancipation. They speak, it is true, to persons for whom the conception of salvation has lost its ancient theological meaning, but who labor nevertheless with the same eternal human difficulty. *Things are wrong with them*; and 'What shall I do to be clear, right, sound, whole, well?' is the form of their question. And the answer is: 'You *are* well, sound, and clear already, if you did but know it.' 'The whole matter may be summed up in one sentence,' says one of the authors whom I have already quoted, '*God is well, and so are you*. You must awaken to the knowledge of your real being'" (108, his emphases).

Noting that the earlier gospels of Luther and Wesley were successful because they addressed the "mental needs" of a large segment of their contemporaries, "Exactly the same adequacy holds in the case of the mind-cure message, foolish as it may sound upon its surface; and seeing its rapid growth in influence, and its therapeutic triumphs, one is tempted to ask whether it may not be destined (probably by very reason of the crudity and extravagance of many of its manifestations) to play a part almost as great in the evolution of the popular religion of the future as did those earlier movements in their day" (108). James takes particular interest in Henry Wood's claim that "nothing but the boundless divine love" is able to "neutralize" the fear that is stamped upon every human before they enter the outer world, holding them in "bondage" throughout their lives. Indeed, for Wood, the boundless love of God has already neutralized this ocean of fear "which has engulfed you and reduced your life [to] a perpetual nightmare" (99).

James's sympathy for Wood's view that the neutralizing of fear depends not on human will but on the boundless divine love is rooted in his own experience of panic fear, noted above. He considered this experience to have "a religious bearing" because "the fear was so invasive and powerful" that if he had not clung to consoling scripture texts he would have grown really insane. In the very throes of a fear so invasive and powerful, he felt at some deep subliminal level the care and protection of the divine. In these straits, fearing for his very sanity, there was nothing he could do for himself but, as Wood put it, "to awaken to the knowledge of [his] real being, which is that of a self who is well because God is well." I will return to this point about the boundless love of God when I discuss Kohut's concept of "the calming structure."

In his later chapter in *The Varieties* on saintliness, James focuses on the "higher nature" of the human individual and discusses several of the "inner conditions" that may become habitual in a person of religious temperament. The most important of these inner conditions is the sense of "a higher and friendly power" (274). The authors he quotes in connection with this inner sense of an "enveloping friendliness" that is "most personal and definite" testify to its power to dispel fear. For example, James cites "an excellent description of this state of mind" from a sermon by Mr. Voysey who declared: "It is the experience of myriads of trustful souls, that this sense of God's unfailing presence with them in their going out and in their coming in, and by night and day, is a source of absolute repose and confident calmness. It drives away all fear of what may befall them. That nearness of God is a constant security against terror and anxiety" (275). Another author, C. H. Hilty, whose book on happiness James cites several times in *The Varieties*, has this to say: "The compensation for the loss of that sense of personal independence which man so unwillingly gives up, is the disappearance of all *fear* from one's life, the quite indescribable and inexplicable feeling of an inner *security*, which one can only experience, but which, once it has been experienced, one can never forget" (275). Thus, both authors emphasize that the presence of God dispels anxieties and fears that would otherwise be immobilizing.

James also discusses the practical consequences of the fundamental inner conditions that are integral to the religious temperament. Included among these is "strength of soul." By this he means "the sense of enlargement of life," which is "so uplifting that personal motives and inhibitions, commonly omnipotent, become too insignificant for notice, and new reaches of patience and fortitude open out. *Fear and anxieties go, and blissful equanimity takes their place"* (273, my emphasis). Later in the same chapter, he declares that the "transition from tenseness, self-responsibility, and worry, to equanimity, receptivity, and peace, is the most wonderful of all those shiftings of inner equilibrium, those changes of the personal center of energy, which I have analyzed so often; and the chief wonder of it is that it so often comes about, not by doing, but by simply relaxing and throwing the burden down" (289). He suggests that this "abandonment of self-responsibility seems to be the fundamental act in specifically religious, as distinguished from moral practice. It antedates theologies and is independent of philosophies. Mind-cure, theosophy, stoicism, ordinary neurological hygiene, insist on it as emphatically as Christianity does, and it is capable of entering into closest marriage with every speculative creed" (289). He adds, "Christians who have it strongly live in what is called 'recollection,' and are never anxious about the future, nor worry over the outcome of the day." He cites Saint Catherine of Genoa, of whom it was said that "she took cognizance of things, only as they were presented to her in succession, moment by moment." To her, "the divine moment was the present moment and when the present moment was estimated in itself and in its relations, and when the duty that was involved in it was accomplished, it was permitted to pass away as if it had never been, and to give way to the facts and duties of the moment which came after" (289).

This illustration from Saint Catherine's life addresses the central feature of social phobia—anxiety, or the anticipation of ordeals that are yet to come—and reflects Jesus' admonitions: "So do not worry about tomorrow, for tomorrow will bring worries of its own" (Matt. 6:34) and "Consider the lilies of the field, how they grow; they neither toil nor spin, yet, I tell you, even Solomon in all his glory was not clothed like one of these" (Matt. 6:28–29). Living in a shame-honor society, Jesus was most likely addressing an audience whose anxiety related not only to matters of physical and economic security, but also concern or dread regarding a future social experience where one anticipates the negative judgments of others. But more important than these circumstantial similarities between Jesus' contemporaries and social phobics is the inner condition that social phobics share with Jesus' contemporaries, an anxiety deriving from the mistaken belief that one must rely solely on herself to get through the ordeals that make her fearful and anxious. In effect, the mind-curers that James quotes were drawing on Jesus' assurances, which were based on his own profound sense of the presence of his heavenly Father, a "higher and friendly power" who anticipates human needs in much the same way that humans anticipate future ordeals. If this "higher and friendly power" feeds the birds of the air and clothes the grass of the field, "Are you not of more value than they?" (Matt. 6:26).

In short, James's discussion of fear in *The Varieties* identifies a key feature of the religious temperament that confronts the anxiety and fear endemic to social phobia. This is the sense of the presence of a higher and friendly power, which establishes and undergirds a "quite indescribable and inexplicable feeling of an inner security" (275). Its practical consequences are a "strength of soul" that views the inhibitions that plague the social phobic—seemingly so omnipotent—as "too insignificant for notice" (273). This religious perspective, however, raises psychodynamic issues that James does not directly address. While he says that a "shifting of inner equilibrium" and "changes of the personal center of energy" occur as a result of this new enveloping presence around and within the self, he does not specify what has actually occurred psychodynamically. Heinz Kohut's concept of "the calming structure" provides an answer.

Heinz Kohut and the Calming Structure

James's discussion of the enveloping presence of the divine suggests that religion addresses the psychodynamic need for what Kohut calls "the transmutation of a structural deficit," namely, a "deficiency in calming structures" (1984, 30). As we have seen, Zerbe suggests that the *therapist* may provide the social phobic patient a "calming structure" during the course of therapy. The social phobic, however, may require this "calming structure" when there is no one present on whom he may rely. Social phobics typically feel that no other human person can provide the support they need in anxious situations. Even the most supportive human "other" is typically perceived to be "one of them" and thus silently judgmental. This is true even when the "other" protests to the contrary and the social phobic "knows" the factual, objective truth of such protestations. Thus, the social phobic may be helped by the "calming structure" that religion provides, of "an all encompassing, enveloping friendliness" that is also "most personal and definite." This calming structure offers, as Voysey puts it, "a *constant* security against terror and anxiety" (my emphasis).

I have referred to Jesus' testimony to the calming structure provided by the enveloping presence of the divine: "Do not be anxious..." "Consider the lilies of the field..." But what of Jesus himself? How can he be a living resource for the social phobic? How can he, a holy man who lived in Palestine some two thousand years ago, make a significant difference in the life of a present day social phobic? To address this question, I will discuss Kohut's concepts of the self and the "selfobject" in greater detail than was possible in the chapter on psychotherapeutic treatment methods. The key to Kohut's self theory is the "nuclear self," which is "that continuum in time, that cohesive configuration in depth, which we experience as the 'I' of our perceptions, thoughts and actions" (Kohut 1985, 9). There are other aspects of the self, but the nuclear self comprises one's central purposes and self-assertive goals and ambitions on the one hand, and one's central idealized values on the other. The nuclear self is not immutable. Its ambitions and values are continually being modified in the course of a lifetime, especially at certain developmental junctures or under the influence of crucial environmental changes. Nonetheless, it is that "cohesive configuration in depth" that we experience as the "I" of our perceptions, thoughts, and actions (11).

Kohut's concept of the selfobject is directly related to the nuclear self. Originally, the child looked to others, especially parents, to affirm her self-assertive ambitions and to inspire her idealized values. But, in time, another process began to replace this exclusive reliance on parental figures for the maintenance of the nuclear self. This was the development of the self's relationship to itself by means of internalized selfobjects. Other persons, especially parents, are the source of selfobjects, but once the internalization process begins, these selfobjects exist independently of the child's image of her mother and father and her actual relationship with them. Selfobjects are integral to the child's "I-ness" and are internalized images of what the child, in her idealizations, perceives herself to be.

In an interview, Kohut discusses the fact that he experiences himself as the same person he was as a small boy even though he has undergone considerable changes over the course of his lifetime: "I'm an old man. My hair is grey. My muscles are feeble. Yet I know I am the same person I was when I was 18, and 22, and 6, when I was running and jumping. It's still in me and a part of me. There is no discontinuity. I have totally changed and yet my conviction that I have remained the same is absolute. I never feel myself chopped up in that way, however otherwise my self might be endangered" (Kohut, 1985, 236). He notes that the little 6-year-old Austrian boy he once was is more similar to little Austrian boys today than to himself, a 68-year-old man, but this 6-year-old boy "isn't somebody else. I'm not estranged from that. I may not remember much about the boy anymore, but he is still with me" (237). Then he added, "It is this sense of continuity, this indefinite sameness, identity, unalterableness that I believe selfobjects respond to" (237).

Kohut's comments on his own nuclear self and its selfobjects occurred in the context of a discussion of cultural selfobjects, that is, of well-known historical figures who are sources for the self-assertive ambitions and idealized values of others. In this discussion, he noted the importance of cultural selfobjects for developing and maintaining a group's nuclear self (e.g., Jackie Robinson and Jesse Owens for the American black community in the 1950s). I suggest that Jesus, especially in the Christian West, functions as a cultural selfobject—one, however, having culturally transcendent qualities—and is therefore an *enduring* source of self-assertive ambitions and idealized values. Viewed thus, he is one whom social phobics, even today, may internalize as a personal selfobject. As such, he is able to help them in their struggles with a pathology that inhibits the realization of their ambitions and goals in life and he enables them to live their lives in fuller consonance with their idealized values. In this sense, he becomes one who not only testifies to the calming presence of the divine, but who also lives *within* the socially phobic individual, as an internalized selfobject, and is therefore integral to the calming structure that the social phobic has been longing for, perhaps since birth.

What, precisely, does it mean to say that Jesus may be integral to the calming structure itself? This question requires that we give attention to Kohut's idea of the calming structure. Kohut discusses the calming structure in his consideration of a case of agoraphobia (1984), which he attributes to "a structural deficiency of the self" (30). He notes that the traditional psychoanalytic view would be that the patient's panic attacks are "no more than a symptom, and the relief the patient experiences when she is accompanied by a woman, in particular an older woman, is no more than a defensive maneuver" (28). The traditional view would further propose that this maneuver is "understandable as an enactment of the mother's presence," which "makes the fulfillment of [the patient's] oedipal desires impossible," thus short-circuiting her oedipal fantasies (i.e., her sexual wishes for her father) and forestalling the outbreak of anxiety (28). Kohut, however, believes that "the agoraphobic woman's essential illness is not defined by her unconscious wish

for incestuous relations with her father and by her unconscious conflicts over them, but by the fact that she suffers from a structural deficiency of the self" (29).

In his view, the woman suffered a "breakup of the self" in early
childhood, and this accounts "for both the disintegration of the agoraphobic woman's affectionate attitude toward the father in childhood
(with pathogenic sexual fantasies replacing the former joyful warmth)
and the tendency toward the spreading of anxiety and development of
paralyzing panic" (30). Thus, it is "the faultily responsive *paternal* selfobject that accounts for the first aspect of the structural disease of the
self (i.e., the ascendency of an Oedipus complex) and the faultily responsive *maternal* selfobject that accounts for the second aspect (i.e.,
the patient's tendency to become overwhelmed by panic rather than
being able to control her anxiety" (30). In effect, the mother "was apparently not able to provide a calming selfobject milieu for the little girl
which, via optimal failures, would have been transmuted into self-
soothing structures capable of preventing the spread of anxiety. It is
this structural deficit, the deficiency in calming structures—a defect in
the soothing functions of the idealized pole of the self—that necessi-
tates the presence of a companion (a maternal woman who temporarily
replaces the missing structure and its functions) to forestall the outbreak of anxiety" (30). Therefore, "It was the nonempathic selfobject
milieu of the oedipal phase" that "both brought about the deleterious
transformation of the little girl's originally affectionate attitudes into
sexual drivenness and failed to provide the necessary conditions for
the gradual internalization of those self structures that would have given
self-confidence to the little girl and enabled her to remain calm despite
conflict and tension" (30).

Thus, Kohut is arguing that the girl's "pathogenic sexual fantasies"
centering on her father are symptomatic of something deeper, a structural deficit in the self. This deficit is primarily due to the absence of a
maternal selfobject (or internalized mother) who is able to give cre-
dence to the girl's need for self-idealization. The little girl needs to be
able to idealize her mother and thereby realize the necessary "calming
selfobject milieu" that enables her to believe in herself. This requires
that the mother is able to be an empathic presence for the girl.

To illustrate his concept of the calming structure, Kohut cites the
example of German Chancellor Otto von Bismarck's severe and chronic
insomnia. Dr. Schweninger, considered a quack by the German medical profession of his day, was called in: "Schweninger, whose intuitive
grasp of the nature of Bismarck's sleep disturbance anticipated some

of the essential insights of psychoanalytic selfpsychology, came to Bismarck's house at bedtime one evening and sat next to the statesman's bed until he had fallen asleep. When Bismarck awakened the next morning, after a full night's sleep, Schweninger was still sitting at his bedside, welcoming him, as it were, into the new day. I believe it would be difficult to find a more striking clinical instance demonstrating how, via a transference enactment, the fulfillment of a patient's need for an empathically responsive selfobject can restore the patient's ability to fall asleep" (19–20). Schweninger responded to Bismarck's "need for a soothing idealized selfobject."

Kohut notes, however, that Schweninger provided a psychotherapeutic cure but not a truly psychoanalytic one. For the latter to happen, it would be necessary to interpret and work through Bismarck's emotional response to Schweninger's presence, perhaps tracing it to a deficit caused by the absence of a maternal selfobject when Bismarck was a small boy. Because this did not occur, Schweninger became an indispensible member of Bismarck's entourage: "He continued, in other words, to serve as Bismarck's selfobject instead of bringing about the increase of the new or reinforced psychic structure that would have given Bismarck the ability to sooth himself into falling asleep with the aid of other selfobjects he would have to provide for himself" (20).

In proposing that Jesus may serve a similar function to the one Schweninger served for Bismarck, I may, admittedly, be inviting the same problem, that is, an *inappropriate* dependence on a religious selfobject who is integral to the calming structure of God. In the course of the following discussion, however, I hope to establish that Jesus—unlike Bismarck's Schweninger—may become a source of genuine empowerment in social contexts where the social phobic feels threatened (caused mainly by their dominance/submissiveness dynamics). Jesus may be, as it were, not so much a means to enable the social phobic to fall asleep at night, but to accompany her—as companion—in those daytime situations that have caused her to experience a debilitating, disempowering anxiety.

Would the presence of Jesus as an internalized selfobject enable the social phobic to enter any and all anxiety-arousing situations? Practically speaking, I doubt it. There are, after all, innate temperamental factors in social phobia that even seismic shiftings of "inner equilibrium" cannot displace. Whatever strength of soul the social phobic comes to possess, this is unlikely to alter his innate temperament, the behavioral inhibition or shyness that has shadowed him from birth. Furthermore, the very idea that the *religious* selfobject would be employed to alter or even destroy the *innate* temperament of the social phobic is a misuse of the gift that religion brings to the life of the social phobic. This very idea flies in the face of the truth that religious change occurs through yielding, by accepting the assurance that "you are well, sound, and clear already, if you did but know it." It is not a matter of changing one's innate temperament but of awakening "to the knowledge of your real being" (James 1982, 108). Accepting the fact of one's innate temperament—in this case, of shyness or behavioral inhibition— is critical to the religious experience of many others (such as lesbian women and gay men) for whom innate characteristics originally considered evidence of a flawed self are no longer considered evidence *against* the self-affirmation that "I am well, sound, and clear already." If anyone can yield to the knowledge that the attempt to change one's innate temperament is an act of hubris, of misguided pride, surely it would be the social phobic, who has a personal history of submissive behavior.

Of course, there are other figures—besides Jesus—in the Christian tradition and in other religious traditions who may also function as internalized objects for social phobics. One thinks here of the whole tradition of Christian saints, several of whom James cites as persons who exhibited great strength of soul. But Jesus is an especially viable self-object for social phobics, perhaps even those who do not identify with the Christian tradition, because he addressed the core issue that threatens their well-being, that of immobilizing fear. Despite their differences, the New Testament gospels testify that Jesus brought a message of hope to persons who were afraid, who lived in mortal fear, in dread of what might befall them. We have already noted his admonition, "So do not worry about tomorrow, for tomorrow will bring worries of its own," and the illustration he offered from the lilies of the field who neither toil nor spin, yet "even Solomon in all his glory was not clothed like one of these." There is also his assurance, "Blessed are the meek, for they will inherit the earth" (Matthew 5:5). What could be more inspiring of social phobics' self-assertive ambitions and idealized values than to be assured that they will be able to roam freely about the social world, treating it as their own?

Jesus recognized that people lived in continual fear of economic catastrophe. Witness, for example, his story of the man who built large barns to store his grain (Luke 12:16–20). The story he tells about the servant who buried the one talent his master had given him to invest (Matthew 25:14–30; Luke 19:12–17) is especially instructive, however, because it concerns the dominance/submissiveness dynamic in social relations. As the servant tried to explain to his master when he returned from his travels and demanded an accounting of what the three servants had done with the money entrusted to them, "Master I knew that you were a harsh man, reaping where you did not sow, and gathering where you did not winnow; *so I was afraid*, and I went and hid your talent in the ground. Here you have what is yours" (Matthew 25:24–25, my emphasis).

This parable suggests that one should not live in fear of what the dominant group—represented by the "harsh" master—may do to him. Instead, one should set aside such fear, as well as the prudence that goes with it, and act more boldly and self-confidently. Why? Not because he has misconstrued the dominant group in viewing them as harsh and unfeeling, but because he can act cautiously, prudently, and circumspectly with those who are dominant *and still be subject to punishment and retribution*. If this is how things are, he may as well set aside his fear of the dominant group and act more boldly, disregarding the consequences.

Another point that Jesus makes regarding the dominant group is that one is not required to accord them any special recognition or deference. This is because those who view Jesus as their teacher in the conduct of their lives recognize God as the one who has "rule" over them. Therefore, Jesus legitimates the refusal to be deferential to whoever may constitute the dominant group in one's own circumstances. His assurance that one need not be anxious or worry about anything because "your father knows that you need these things" is followed by the simple injunction, "Instead, make sure of his rule over you, and all these things will be yours as well" (Mack 1993, 78).

In short, the social phobic who has Jesus as her internalized selfobject—and as more integral to the calming structure of God than any other—does not enter feared social situations alone. Rather, she enters them with an internalized other who legitimates her presence in the company of those she fears. This internalized selfobject is not numbered among those who are the dominant ones, whose negative judgments and condemning attitudes are feared. Instead, he is the quiet, assuring voice inside the social phobic, reminding her that there is nothing to fear because the power she has attributed to the dominant class is empty, null, and void. This is a very different way of "restructuring" one's assumptions and beliefs about the feared situation than that of the cognitive-behavioral therapists. These therapists encourage the socially anxious person to consider whether he has rational grounds for believing that he is as subject to negative judgment as he thinks he is, and they assume that he does not. Thus, cognitive-behavioral therapy is based on a rather benign view of the social world. In contrast, Jesus emphasizes that the social world is, in fact, comprised of critics, judges, and detractors. Yet, in spite of this, he advocates involvement in this world on the grounds that the power of the dominant group is for the time being and will soon pass away. In addition, he embodies that which *is* benign, that is, the enveloping presence of God.

I realize that cognitive-behavioral therapy has provided evidence that the social world is not as judgmental as the social phobic believes it to be. The simulated role-play technique commonly used in cognitive-behavioral therapy helps the client to see that her audience is not nearly as prone to criticize her social performance as she assumes. We should not forget, however, that the group in these simulated cases is comprised of other social phobics who share a common plight and are therefore strongly disposed to treat each other with considerable kindness and mutual concern. The therapeutic group represents an ideal in human civility that is rarely found in real-life social interaction.

A truer view of the social context, especially its capacity to injure, is provided by the classic case of social phobia in the Bible: the prophet Jonah. Jonah knew that the Ninevites had both the ability and the will to make a fool of him. He therefore tried to avoid going to Ninevah. When he eventually went, things turned out much as he had expected. By repenting, the Ninevites succeeded in humiliating him (proving his prophecy wrong). How did Jonah know in advance that they would do this to him? I believe that his prescience was partly due to the fact that he had experienced other situations in the past in which either he or someone else was the victim of a similar social injury. I would also surmise that it stemmed from the fact that, when in situations where *he* was not the center of attention, he had not hesitated to be critical of the performance of those who were. As the preacher in Ecclesiastes writes, "Do not give heed to everything that people say, or you may hear your servant cursing you; your heart knows that many times you have yourself cursed others" (7:21–22). The social phobic is especially sensitive to the fact that negative judgments are being made in social contexts, and that it is unrealistic to believe that there is any social situation in which such judgments are not being made. Social phobics are perhaps more realistic in this regard than therapists who—perhaps more often members of the dominant group—may assume that social situations are more benign then they actually are.

Jesus' own view of the social situation as always reflective of a dominance/submissiveness dynamic is also realistic. Thus, his assurance that one has nothing to fear is not based on any naive belief in the benign nature of human interaction, but on the conviction that the power the dominant group derives from the collusion of the submissive group is extremely tenuous. In most situations, the submissives have the ultimate power of withdrawing from or otherwise avoiding situations in which they are likely to be victimized by those who are dominant. In this sense, the social phobic's avoidant behavior may be an act of protest. The social phobic who avoids an especially threatening situation is often secretly admired by those who believed that they had no choice but to attend and be subjected to demeaning or self-aggrandizing behavior by the dominant group. In situations where the social phobic finds it impossible *not* to be physically present, she may silently protest being dominated by the group's leaders by choosing not to listen to what they have to say and failing to pay attention to what they are doing.

As an internalized selfobject, Jesus validates such overt or covert acts of protest against the dominant group. He supports the refusal—through such acts of silent protest—to collude against oneself. In this sense, he becomes the social phobic's advocate. Such advocacy is reflected, for example, in his defense of the woman who was accused of being an adulteress and was about to be stoned by her accusers (John 8:1–11). As Joplin (1992) points out in her analysis of the story, he took responsibility for the resolution of this social crisis, linking his fate to hers. If he failed to condemn her, he would seem to violate Mosaic law, but if he did condemn her, he would violate Roman law, for in this period of Jewish-Roman relations, it was believed that the Sanhedrin's power to levy a death sentence was removed by Roman decree. He evaded this carefully constructed double bind—his entrapment between two laws, one religious and one secular—in a way that no one expected (229–230). He declared to the crowd, "If there is one of you who has not sinned, let him be the first to throw a stone at her." As he wrote on the ground in silence, each member of the crowd began to look into his own conscience. Beginning with the elders, the crowd began to disperse. Thus, he undermined the apparent differences between the righteous men and the guilty woman. By challenging her accusers, even insinuating that the man—or men—with whom she had committed adultery were among her crowd of accusers, he created a social situation in which no one present would exempt himself from self-judgment. What Jesus had done was "to reconstitute the missing [or hidden] adulterer by locating him in the conscience of every male present" (233).

Jesus demonstrated through his advocacy role that the dominant group had no power over the woman. With Jesus present, incongruously writing in silence on the ground after issuing his challenge, the power of her accusers was nullified. This very Jesus, the one who undermines the prevailing dominance/submissiveness dynamics in a social situation, is accessible to the social phobic in the form of an internalized selfobject. As selfobject, he continues to enact his role as the healer of human spirits burdened with anxiety and fear. Against the "automatic thoughts" with which social phobics anticipate feared social situations, he offers these words of assurance and empowerment: "Blessed are the meek, for they will inherit the earth" (Matthew 5:5). In behalf of the social phobic, he envisions the day when they will enter any and all social situations they have heretofore avoided. For those who experience within themselves his empowering, subversive presence, this vision is already a discernible reality.

Conclusion

In the conclusion to the preceding chapter on cultural differences, I suggested that Okano's principle of flexibility may be used to support the social phobic's right to decide to enter certain feared situations and avoid others. Here I have suggested that there are two ways in which religion may help to alleviate the social phobic's anxieties and fears whatever the decision and its outcome may be.

One is that the social phobic may cultivate a deeper awareness of the calming presence of God. Against his natural tendency to believe that he must rely solely upon himself to survive social situations that are anxiety arousing, he may adopt the belief that he has a "higher and friendly power" who is present to him. This calming presence of God does not ensure a "successful" immersion in the feared situation, as though God were her insurance of performing well. Rather, the calming presence of God enables her to believe that success or failure is not the issue. This is because the social situation is no longer ascribed the power to determine what makes for failure or success. Even if she feels she has failed by leaving the feared social situation too early or revealing her distress during the presentation of the speech or report, the calming presence of God remains with her after the dreaded event and assures her that there was no failure in the eyes of the One whose opinion alone matters. The divine does not say, "I love your 'successful' self but I despise your 'failing' self." Rather, the failing self is precisely the one to whom God reaches out and embraces as God's very own. As the social phobic enters a situation that makes him anxious, God's calming presence allows him to believe that he has no reason to be anxious: Consider the lilies of the field, the birds of the air. If God upholds them, will God not also uphold you and keep you from falling? And, as she leaves a situation feeling she has not done her best, feeling disappointed and letdown by her own performance, the calming presence of God allows her to believe that she is well, saved, and clear already. What happened in there—at the party, in the classroom, in the meeting room, in the auditorium, in the boss's office, at the sales counter—was not without its significance, but it was not a defeat, because it was not, after all, a reflection of her true inner worth.

Such cultivation of the calming presence of God does not entail the grandiose belief that because God is with me, I can totally overcome my fears and enter into any and all social situations with assurance and confidence. The calming presence of God is not about becoming fearless or about being a model of self-assurance. In fact, were one able to become such, he would endanger what has become precious to him, the calming presence of God, the sense that he is never alone, even in situations where he feels conspicuous and experiences himself as being under the critical, judging gaze of others. The point is not that she need no longer exercise discernment concerning which situations she will enter into and which she will choose to avoid, but that she is accompanied by the calming structure of God's presence whenever she enters situations that cause her to be anxious. Psalm 131 beautifully expresses this understanding of the calming presence of God:

> O Lord, *my heart is not lifted up,*
> *my eyes are not raised too high;*
> *I do not occupy myself with things*
> *too great and too marvelous for me.*
> *But I have calmed and quieted my soul,*
> *like a child quieted at its mother's breast;*
> *like a child that is quieted is my soul. (RSV)*

This decision to avoid occupying herself with "things too great and too marvelous for me" is not weakness. Rather, it reflects her strength of soul, which, in turn, has its basis in the calming presence of God. Such strength of soul enables her to forgo dreams of being a great public orator, a persuasive voice in a committee discussion of an important policy issue, a bright and witty conversationalist, an accomplished self-promoter who is able to get the boss to endorse her every whim. This does not mean, however, that he is bereft or demoralized, for what he has instead is a strength of soul that is, in its own paradoxical way, a source of empowerment.

This reliance on the calming presence of God has certain affinities with relaxation methods. It is more fundamentally congruent, however, with the cognitive treatment approach, which emphasizes that our beliefs make a difference in how we experience a given social situation. Awareness of the calming presence of God before, during, and after the feared social situation relativizes the social phobic's conditional beliefs concerning social evaluation and dramatically alters unconditional beliefs about the self. It replaces views of himself as "incompetent" and "socially inept" with a core conviction that "I am well, sound, and clear already." No single social situation, however negatively evaluated he feels (by others and himself), has the power to dislodge this fundamental core conviction.

The psychoanalytic approach to social phobia is also relevant because it emphasizes that phobias develop, in part, because an adequate calming structure did not form in early childhood. In light of this, we should note that Psalm 131 employs the metaphor of the child resting peacefully at her mother's breast and represents the poet's soul as "a child who is quieted." If this means that the calming presence of God is a surrogate, as it were, for the calming structure of the child's mother, we should welcome this thought, because there is a profoundly maternal aura to the perception that God is present before, during, and subsequent to the dreaded social ordeal, or in the wake of self-recriminations for the decision to avoid it.

The second resource religion provides the social phobic is of Jesus as the one who goes with her into perilous social situations. As one who challenged the power of the dominant group to injure the submissive ones, he is an inner source of self-empowerment. He is the one who enables the social phobic to disregard the power of the dominant ones—to enter the situations that others control—in a spirit of quiet defiance, knowing that she need not give them what they want, that she may act in a manner that appears "submissive" but is in fact a refusal to be moved. Herein lies the basic paradox of social phobia, namely, that social phobics are so well schooled in the art of submissiveness that they are able to adopt a pseudo-submissiveness that completely disarms—even, at times, completely fools—the dominant group. Thus, the empowerment that Jesus offers is remarkably resonant with the traditional Japanese belief that power is not in what is revealed but in what is concealed. As Joplin notes, there has been a great deal of speculation about what Jesus was writing on the ground while the fate of the adulteress hung in the balance (231). Whatever it may have been, the gospel writer concealed it from his readers. In such concealment lies much of the power of the story. In a similar way, the social phobic's power consists in the fact that his submissiveness may—or may not—be what it seems. As an internalized selfobject, Jesus validates this concealment. The very fact that this selfobject accompanies the social phobic into potentially perilous situations is, after all, itself a matter of concealment, of unrevealed power.

Except for the fact that this recommendation is theoretically supported by the Kohutian idea of the internalized selfobject, there is little in the treatment literature on social phobia that anticipates it. This is partly because the literature emphasizes the solitariness of the social phobic and develops its own recommendations with this solitariness in view. As we have seen, the one treatment plan that advocates the therapist's own participation with the phobic person (the self-efficacy model) was designed mainly for specific phobias and agoraphobia and, for reasons cited, appears to be much less effective in the case of social phobia. This emphasis on the solitary individual is also because the treatment literature views the social phobic as the one who has the pathology. Therefore, it tends to view the social context as relatively benign. It seems to say: The social setting is well, sound, and clear, but you are not.

However, like the demon-possessed in Jesus' day whose pathology revealed the fact that the social order itself was demonic (Hollenbach 1976), social phobics have their own judgment to make concerning contemporary social life. They are especially critical of the dominance/submissiveness dimension of contemporary social life and cherish those social situations in which dominance and submission dynamics are minimized and participants relate together as equals. The very fact that social phobics are rarely anxious in situations where dynamics of dominance and submissiveness are minimal (such as harmonious family situations and interaction with close friends) is powerful evidence that social phobia has its own judgment to make against the prevailing social order. The dominance/submissiveness system is unavoidable and has been an aspect of every human society and every group within these societies. It magnifies itself, however, in an age—such as ours—of self-promotion. For social phobics, a truer social order is expressed in the image of "the table of the Lord," the one social setting in which dominance/submissiveness dynamics are out of place. The social phobic would not be anxious there.

For the time being, however, Jesus validates the power of concealment in uncomfortable situations. He also validates the decision to take
our leave of such situations when it becomes clear that the dominant
group has invalidated *itself*. As William Stafford's poem, "Freedom of
Expression," puts it (1996, 72):

> My feet wait there listening, and when
> they dislike what happens they begin
> to press on the floor. They know when
> it is time to walk out on a program. Pretty
> soon
> they are moving, and as the program fades
> you can hear the sound of my feet on gravel.
>
> If you have feet with standards, you too
> may be reminded—you need not
> accept what's given. You gamblers,
> pimps, braggarts, oppressive people:—
> "Not here," my feet are saying, "no thanks;
> let me out of this." And I'm gone.

The same Jesus who told his disciples to shake the dust of an
unwelcoming village off their feet helps us determine when it is time to
take our leave.

References

Akillas, E., & Efran, J. S. (1995) Symptom prescription and reframing: Should they be combined? *Cognitive Therapy and Research*, 19:263–79.

American Psychiatric Association (1994). *Diagnostic and Statistical Manual of Mental Disorders (DSM-IV)*. Washington, D.C.: American Psychiatric Association.

Arkin, R. M. (1986). Shyness and self-presentation. In W. H. Jones, J. M. Cheek, & S. R. Briggs, eds., *Shyness: Perspectives on Research and Treatment*. New York: Plenum Press.

Arrindell, W. A. et al. (1989). Perceived parental rearing styles of agoraphobic and socially phobic in-patients. *British Journal of Psychiatry*, 155:526–35.

Baker, S. R., & Boaz, D. (1983). The partial reformation of a traumatic memory of a dental phobia during trance: A case study. *The International Journal of Clinical and Experimental Hypnosis*, 31:14–18.

Bandura, A. et al. (1980). Tests of the generality of self-efficacy theory. *Cognitive Therapy and Research*, 4:39–66.

Beck, A. T. et al. (1979). *Cognitive Therapy of Depression: A Treatment Manual*. New York: The Guilford Press.

Beck, A. T. et al. (1985). *Anxiety Disorders and Phobias: A Cognitive Perspective*. New York: Basic Books.

Beidel, D. C., & Morris, T. L. (1995). Social phobia. In J. S. March, ed. *Anxiety Disorders in Children and Adolescents*. New York: The Guilford Press, 181–211.

Bergmann, M. V. (1980). On the genesis of narcissistic and phobic character formation in an adult patient: A developmental view. *International Journal of Psychoanalysis*, 61:535–46.

Bourdon, K. H. et al. (1988). Gender differences in phobias: Results of the ECA community survey. *Journal of Anxiety Disorders*, 2:227–41.

Breuer, J., & Freud, S. (1955). Studies on hysteria. In J. Strachey, ed. and trans.,*The Standard Edition of the Complete Psychological Works of Sigmund Freud*, 2. London: Hogarth Press, 1–311. Originally published in 1893–1895.

Brown, D. R. et al. (1990). Racial differences in prevalence of phobic disorders. *The Journal of Nervous and Mental Disease*, 178:434–41.

Bruch, M. A., & Cheek, J. M. (1995). Developmental factors in childhood and adolescent shyness. In R. G. Heimberg et al., eds., *Social Phobia: Diagnosis, Assessment, and Treatment*. New York: The Guilford Press, 163–82.

Bruch, M. A., & Heimberg, R. G. (1994). Differences in perceptions of parental and personal characteristics between generalized and nongeneralized social phobics. *Journal of Anxiety Disorders*, 8:155–168.

Bruch, M. et al. (1989). Social phobia and perceptions of early parental and personal characteristics. *Anxiety Research*, 2:57–65.

Buss, A. H. (1980). *Self-Consciousness and Social Anxiety*. San Francisco, Calif.: Freeman Press.

Buss, A. H. (1986). A theory of shyness. In W. H. Jones, J. M. Cheek, & S. R. Briggs, eds., *Shyness: Perspectives on Research and Treatment*. New York: Plenum Press.

Butler, G. (1985). Exposure as a treatment for social phobia: Some instructive difficulties. *Behavior Research and Therapy*, 23:651–657.

Butler, G., & Wells, A. (1995). Cognitive-behavioral treatments: Clinical applications. In R. G. Heimberg et al., eds., *Social Phobia: Diagnosis, Assessment, and Treatment*. New York: The Guilford Press, pp. 310–33.

Chaleby, K. (1987). Social phobia in Saudis. *Social Psychiatry*, 22:167–170.

Chapman, T. F. et al. (1995). Epidemiology and family studies of social phobia. In R. G. Heimberg et al., eds., *Social Phobia: Diagnosis, Assessment, and Treatment*. New York: The Guilford Press, 21–40.

Clark, D. M., & Wells, A. (1995). A cognitive model of social phobia. In R.G. Heimberg et al., eds., *Social Phobia: Diagnosis, Assessment, and Treatment*. New York: The Guilford Press, 69–93.

Coleman, M. D. (1982/1983). Prestructuring determinants in a case of phobia. *International Journal of Psychoanalytical Psychotherapy*, 9:537–51.

Cook, E. W. et al. (1988). Emotional imagery and the differential diagnosis of anxiety. *Journal of Consulting and Clinical Psychology*, 56:734–40.

Darwin, C. (1998). *The Expression of the Emotions in Man and Animals*. New York: Oxford University Press.

David, D. et al. (1995). Panic-phobic patients and developmental trauma. *Journal of Clinical Psychiatry*, 56:113–17.

Davidson, J. R. T. et al. (1994). The boundary of social phobia. *Archives of General Psychiatry*, 51:975–83.

Donahue, B. C. et al. (1994). Behavioral assessment and treatment of social phobia: An evaluative review. *Behavior Modification*, 18:262–88.

Elting, D. T., & Hope, D. A. (1995). Cognitive assessment. In R.G. Heimberg et al., eds., *Social Phobia: Diagnosis, Assessment, and Treatment*. New York: The Guilford Press, 232–58.

Fisher, S., & Fisher, R. L. (1993). *The Psychology of Adaptation to Absurdity: Tactics of Make-Believe.* Hillsdale, N.J.: Lawrence Erlbaum Associates.

Frankl, V. E. (1939). Zur medikamentösen Unterstützung der Psychotherapie bei Neurosen. *Schweizer Archiv für Neurologie und Psychiatrie*, 43:26–31.

Frankl, V. E. (1975). Paradoxical intention and dereflection. *Psychotherapy: Theory, Research and Practice*, 12:226–37.

Freud, S. (1961). The Ego and the Id. In J. Strachey, ed. and trans., *The Standard Edition of the Complete Psychological Works of Sigmund Freud*, 7. London: Hogarth Press, 123–245. Originally published in 1923.

Fyer, A. J. et al. (1993). A direct interview family study of social phobia. *Archives of General Psychiatry*, 50:286–93.

Gabbard, G. O. (1992). Psychodynamics of panic disorder and social phobia. *Bulletin of the Menninger Clinic*, 56:A3–A13.

Gambrill, E. (1995). Helping shy, socially anxious, and lonely adults: A skill-based contextual approach. In W. O'Donahue & L. Krasner, eds., *Handbook of Psychological Skills Training: Clinical Techniques and Applications*. Boston: Allyn & Bacon, 247–86.

Ghosh, A., & Marks, I. M. (1987). Self-treatment of agoraphobia by exposure. *Behavior Therapy*, 18:3–16.

Greist, J. H. (1995). The diagnosis of social phobia. *Journal of Clinical Psychiatry*, 56 (Suppl. 5): 5–12.

Haley, J. (1973). *Uncommon Therapy: The Psychiatric Techniques of Milton H. Erickson, M.D.* New York: W. W. Norton.

Hand, I., & Lamontagne, Y. (1976). The exacerbation of interpersonal problems after rapid phobia-removal. *Psychotherapy: Theory, Research and Practice*, 13:405–11.

Hayes, S. C., & Barlow, D. H. (1977). Flooding relief in a case of public transportation phobia. *Behavioral Therapy*, 8:742–46.

Heckelman, L. R., & Schneier, F. R. (1995). Diagnostic issues. In R. G. Heimberg et al., eds., *Social Phobia: Diagnosis, Assessment, and Treatment*. New York: The Guilford Press, 3–20.

Heimberg, R. G., & Barlow, D. H. (1988). Psychosocial treatments for social phobia. *Psychosomatics*, 29:27–37.

Heimberg, R. G., & Juster, H. R. (1994). Treatment of social phobia in cognitive-behavioral groups. *Journal of Clinical Psychiatry*, 55:38–46.

Heimberg, R. G., & Juster, H. R. (1995). Cognitive-behavioral treatments: Literature review. In R. G. Heimberg et al., eds., *Social Phobia: Diagnosis, Assessment, and Treatment*. New York: The Guilford Press, 261–309.

Heimberg, R. G. et al. (1985). Treatment of social phobia by exposure, cognitive restructuring, and homework assignments. *The Journal of Nervous and Mental Disease*, 173:236–45.

Hollenbach, P. W. (1976). Jesus, demoniacs, and public authorities: A socio-historical study. *Journal of the American Academy of Religion*, 44:567–88.

Holt, C. S. et al. (1992). Situational domains of social phobia. *Journal of Anxiety Disorders*, 6:63–77.

Holt, P. E., & Andrews, G. (1989). Provocation of panic: Three elements of the panic reaction in four anxiety disorders. *Behaviour Research and Therapy*, 27:253–61.

Hope, D. A. et al. (1990). Representations of the self in social phobia: Vulnerability to social threat. *Cognitive Therapy and Research*, 14:177–89.

Humphreys, L., & Beiman, I. (1975). The application of multiple behavioral techniques to multiple problems of a complex case. *Journal of Behavior Therapy and ExperimentalPsychiatry*, 6:311–15.

James, W. (1950). *The Principles of Psychology*, 2 vols. New York: Dover Publications. Originally published in 1890.

James, W. (1961). *Psychology: The Briefer Course*. Gordon Allport, ed. Notre Dame, Ind.: University of Notre Dame Press. Originally published in 1892.

James, W. (1982). *The Varieties of Religious Experience*. New York: Penguin Books. Originally published in 1902.

Jansen, M. A. et al. (1994). Personality disorders and features in social phobia and panic disorder. *Journal of Abnormal Psychology*, 103:391–95.

Jarrett, F. J., & Schnurr, R. (1979). Phobias and depression: Clinical and psychometric aspects. *Journal of Behavior Therapy and Experimental Psychiatry*, 10:167–71.

Joplin, P. K. (1992). Intolerable language: Jesus and the woman taken in adultery. In P. Berry and A. Wernick, eds. *Shadow of Spirit: Postmodernism and Religion*. London: Routledge, 227–37.

Kagan, J., & Reznick, S. J. (1986). Shyness and temperament. In W. H. Jones et al., eds., *Shyness: Perspectives on Research and Treatment*. New York: Plenum Press, 81–90.

Kagan, J. et al. (1987). The physiology and psychology of behavioral inhibition in children. *Child Development*, 58:1459–73.

Kaufman, G. (1985). *Shame: The Power of Caring*, 2nd rev. ed. Cambridge, Mass.: Schenkman Books.

Kaufman, G., & L. Raphael (1996). *Coming Out of Shame: Transforming Gay and Lesbian Lives*. New York: Doubleday.

Kessler, M. N. (1995). Will social phobics answer the telephone? *American Journal of Psychiatry*, 152:653.

Kitayama, O. (1985). Pre-oedipal "taboo" in Japanese folk tragedies. *International Journal of Psychoanalysis*, 12:173–86.

Kitayama, O. (1987). Metaphorization-making terms. *International Journal of Psychoanalysis*, 68:499–509.

Knight, J. A. (1967). Church phobia. *Pastoral Psychology*, 18:33–38.

Koenig, H. G. et al. (1993). Religion and anxiety disorder: An examination and comparison of associations in young, middle-aged, and elderly adults. *Journal of Anxiety Disorders*, 7:321– 42.

Kohut, H. (1971). *The Analysis of the Self*. New York: International Universities Press.

Kohut, H. (1977). *The Restoration of the Self*. New York: International Universities Press.

Kohut, H. (1984). *How Does Analysis Cure?* Arnold Goldberg, ed. Chicago: The University of Chicago Press.

Kohut, H. (1985). *Self-Psychology and the Humanities: Reflections on a New Psychoanalytic Approach*. C. Strozier, ed. New York: W. W. Norton.

Lamb, C. S. (1985). Hypnotically-induced deconditioning: Reconstruction of memories in the treatment of phobias. *American Journal of Clinical Hypnosis*, 28:56–62.

Lasch, C. (1979). *The Culture of Narcissism: American Life in an Age of Diminishing Expectations*. New York: W. W. Norton.

Leary, M. R., & Kowalski, R. M. (1995). The self-presentational model of social phobia. In R. G. Heimberg et al., eds., *Social Phobia: Diagnosis, Assessment, and Treatment*. New York: The Guilford Press, 94–112.

Lee, H. B., & Oei, T. P. S. (1994). Factor structure, validity, and reliability of the fear questionnaire in a Hong Kong Chinese population. *Journal of Psychopathology and Behavior Assessment*, 16:189–99.

Lewis, A. (1970). Problems posed by the ambiguous word 'anxiety' as used in psychopathology. *Israel Annals of Psychiatry and Related Disciplines*, 5:105–21.

Lewis, R. W. B. (1991). *The Jameses: A Family Narrative*. New York: Farrar, Straus and Giroux.

Liebowitz, M. R. et al. (1985). Social phobia: Review of a neglected anxiety disorder. *Archives of General Psychiatry*, 42:729–36.

Lindemann, C. (1994). Phobias. In B. B. Wolman & Stricker, G., eds. *Anxiety and Related Disorders: A Handbook*. New York: John Wiley & Sons, 161–76.

Linden, W. (1981). Exposure treatment for focal phobias. *Archives of General Psychiatry*, 38:769–75.

Llewelyn, S. P. (1980). The uses of an eclectic approach: A case study. *British Journal of Medical Pyschology*, 53:145–49.

Lukas, E. (1984). *Meaningful Living: A Logotherapy Guide to Health*. New York: Grove Press.

Lynd, H. M. (1958). *On Shame and the Search for Identity*. New York: Science Editions.

Mack, B. L. (1993). *The Lost Gospel: The Book of Q and Christian Origins*. San Francisco, Calif.: Harper San Francisco.

Mahler, M. S. et al. (1975). *The Psychological Birth of the Human Infant: Symbiosis and Individuation*. New York: Basic Books.

Marks, I. (1995). Advances in behavioral-cognitive therapy of social phobia. *Journal of Clinical Psychiatry*, 56:25–31.

Marks, I. M., & Gelder, M. G. (1966). Different ages of onset in varieties of phobias. *American Journal of Psychiatry*, 123:218–21.

McNeil, D. W. et al. (1995). Behavioral assessment: Self-report, physiology, and overt behavior. In R. G. Heimberg et al., eds., *Social Phobia: Diagnosis, Assessment, and Treatment*. New York: The Guilford Press, 202–31.

Meissner, W. W. et al. (1987). A view of aggression in phobic states. *Psychoanalytic Quarterly*, 56: 452–76.

Menninger, W. W. (1994). Psychotherapy and integrated treatment of social phobia and comorbid conditions. *Bulletin of the Menninger Clinic*, 58: A84–A90.

Mersch, P. P. A. et al. (1992). Somatic symptoms in social phobia: A treatment method based on rational emotive therapy and paradoxical interventions. *Journal of Behavioral Therapy and Experimental Psychiatry*, 23:199–211.

Miller, S. (1985). *The Shame Experience*. Hillsdale, N.J.: Erlbaum.

Mineka S., & Zinbarg, R. (1995). Conditioning and ethological models of social phobia. In R. G. Heimberg et al., eds., *Social Phobia: Diagnosis, Assessment, and Treatment*. New York: The Guilford Press.

Morrison, A. P. (1996). *The Culture of Shame*. New York: Ballantine Books.

Mott, T. (1986). Current status of hypnosis in the treatment of phobias. *American Journal of Clinical Hypnosis*, 28:135–37.

Munjack, D. J., & Moss, H. B. (1981). Affective disorder and alcoholism in families of agoraphobics. *Archives of General Psychiatry*, 38:869–71.

Newell, R., & Shrubb, S. (1994). Attitude change and behavior therapy in dysmorphophobia: Two case reports. *Behavioral and Cognitive Psychotherapy*, 22:163–69.

Öhman, A. (1986). Face the beast and fear the face: Animal and social fears as prototypes for evolutionary analysis of emotion. *Psychophysiology*, 23:123–45.

Okano, K-I. (1994). Shame and social phobia: A transcultural viewpoint. *Bulletin of the Menninger Clinic*, 58:323–38.

Öst, L-G. (1978). Fading: A new technique in the treatment of phobias. *Behavior Research and Therapy*, 16:213–16.

Öst, L-G. (1985). Ways of acquiring phobias and outcome of behavioral treatments. *Behavior Research and Therapy*, 23:683–89.

Öst, L-G. (1987). Age of onset in different phobias. *Journal of Abnormal Psychology*, 96:223–29.

Otto, R. (1923). *The Idea of the Holy*. J. H. Harvey trans. London: Oxford University Press.

Pfister, O. (1948). *Christianity and Fear: A Study in History and in the Psychology and Hygiene of Religion*. W. H. Johnston, trans. London: George Allen & Unwin.

Pollard, C. A. et al. (1989). Help-seeking patterns of anxiety-disordered individuals in the general population. *Journal of Anxiety Disorders*, 3, 131–38.

Pollard, C. A., & Henderson, J. G. (1988). Four types of social phobia in a community sample. *The Journal of Nervous and Mental Disease*, 176: 440–45.

Potts, N. L. S., & Davidson, J. R. T. (1995). Pharmacological treatments: Literature review. In R. G. Heimberg et al., eds., *Social Phobia: Diagnosis, Assessment, and Treatment*. New York: The Guilford Press, 334–65.

Pribor, E. F., & Dinwiddie, S. H. (1992). Psychiatric correlates of incest in childhood. *American Journal of Psychiatry*, 149:52–56.

Pruyser, P. W. (1983). *The Play of the Imagination: Toward a Psychoanalysis of Culture*. New York: International Universities Press.

Quinlan, M. J. (1953). Memoir of William Cowper: An autobiography edited with an introduction. *Proceedings of the American Philosophical Society*, 97:359–82.

Ragsdale, J. E., & Durham, K. R. (1966). Audience response to religious fear appeals. *Review of Religious Research*, 28:40–50.

Rapee, R. M. (1995). Descriptive psychopathology of social phobia. In R. G. Heimberg et al., eds., *Social Phobia: Diagnosis, Assessment, and Treatment*. New York: The Guilford Press, 41–66.

Rapee, R. M., & Lim, L. (1992). Discrepancy between self- and observer ratings of performance in social phobics. *Journal of Abnormal Psychology*, 101:728–31.

Rapee, R. M. et al. (1988). Social phobia features across the *DSM-III-R* anxiety disorders. *Journal of Psychopathology and Behavioral Assessment*, 10:287–99.

Reich, J. (1986). The epidemiology of anxiety. *The Journal of Nervous and Mental Disease*, 174:129–36.

Reich, J. et al. (1988). Anxiety symptoms distinguishing social phobia from panic and generalized anxiety disorders. *The Journal of Nervous and Mental Disease*, 176:510–13.

Rosenbaum, J. F. et al. (1991). Behavioral inhibition in children: A possible precursor to panic disorder or social phobia. *Journal of Clinical Psychiatry*, 55:10–16.

Ross, J. (1980). The use of former phobics in the treatment of phobias. *American Journal of Psychiatry*, 137:715–17.

Ross, J. (1991). Social phobia: The Anxiety Disorders Association of America helps raise the veil of ignorance. *Journal of Clinical Psychiatry*, 52: 43–47.

Roth, M. & Argyle, N. (1988). Anxiety, panic and phobic disorders: An overview. *Journal of Psychiatric Research*, 22:33–54.

Routh, D. K., & Bernholtz, J. E. (1991). Detachment, separation, and phobias. In J. L. Gewirtz & Kurtines, W. M., eds., *Intersections With Attachment*. Hillsdale, N.J.:Lawrence Erlbaum, 295–309.

Salkoviskis, P. M. (1991). The importance of behaviour in the maintenance of anxiety and panic: A cognitive account. *Behavioral Psychotherapy*, 19:6–19.

Schneier, F. R. et al. (1992). Social phobia: Comorbidity and morbidity in an epidemiological sample. *Archives of General Psychiatry*, 49:282–88.

Schneier, F. R. et al. (1994). Functional impairment in social phobia. *Journal of Clinical Psychiatry*, 55:322–31.

Shorkey, C., & Himle, D. P. (1974). Systematic desensitization treatment of a recurring nightmare and related insomnia. *Journal of Behavior Therapy and Experimental Psychiatry*, 5:97–98.

Stafford, W. (1996). *Even in Quiet Places*. Lewiston, Idaho: Confluence Press.

Stein, M. B. et al. (1995). Reply to Mr. Kessler. *American Journal of Psychiatry*, 152:653–54.

Stopa, L., & Clark, D. M. (1993). Cognitive processes in social phobia. *Behavior Research and Therapy*, 31:255–67.

Thyer, B. A. et al. (1988). Is parental death a selective precursor to either panic disorder or agoraphobia? A test of the separation anxiety hypothesis. *Journal of Anxiety Disorders*, 2:333–38.

Tikalsky, F. D., & Wallace, S. D. (1988). Culture and the structure of children's fears. *Journal of Cross-Cultural Psychology*, 19:481–92.

Trower, P., & Gilbert, P., (1989). New theoretical conceptions of social anxiety in clinic and nonclinic samples: Psychological and cognitive correlates. *Journal of Consulting and Clinical Psychology*, 54:523–27.

Turner, S. M. et al. (1986). Psychopathology of social phobia and comparison to avoidant personality disorder. *Journal of Abnormal Psychology*, 95:389–94.

Uhde, T. W. et al. (1991). Phenomenology and neurobiology of social phobia: Comparison with panic disorder. *Journal of Clinical Psychiatry*, 52:31–40.

Van Amerigen, M. (1991). Relationship of social phobia with other psychiatric illness. *Journal of Affective Disorders*, 21:93–99.

Watzlawick, P. et al. (1974). *Change: Principles of Problem Formation and Problem Resolution*. New York: W. W. Norton.

Wells, A. et al. (1995). Social phobia: the role of in-situation safety behaviors in maintaining anxiety and negative beliefs. *Behavior Therapy*, 26:153–61.

Wieselberg, N. et al. (1979). The desensitization derby: *In vivo* down the backstretch, imaginal at the wire? *Journal of Clinical Psychology*, 35: 647–50.

Williams, S. L. (1987). On anxiety and phobia. *Journal of Anxiety Disorders*, 1:161–80.

Williams, S. L. (1988). Addressing misconceptions about phobia, anxiety, and self-efficacy: A reply to Marks. *Journal of Anxiety Disorders*, 2: 277–89.

Williams, S. L. (1992). Perceived self-efficacy and phobic disability. In R. Schwarzer, ed., *Self-Efficacy: Thought Control of Action*. Washington, D.C.: Hemisphere Publishing Corporation, 149–76.

Williams, S. L., & Kleifield, E. (1985). Transfer of behavioral change across phobias in multiple phobic clients. *Behavior Modification*, 9:22–31.

Williams, S. L. et al. (1985). Guided mastery and performance desensitization treatments for severe acrophobia. *Journal of Consulting and Clinical Psychology*, 53:237–47.

Wlazlo, Z. et al. (1990). Exposure *in vivo* vs. social skills training for social phobia: Long-term outcome and differential effects. *Behavior Research and Therapy*, 28:181–93.

Zajecki, J. M., & Ross, J. S. (1995). Management of comorbid anxiety and depression. *Journal of Clinical Psychiatry, 56*:10–13.

Zerbe, K. J. (1994). Uncharted waters: Psychodynamic considerations in the diagnosis and treatment of social phobia. *Bulletin of the Menninger Clinic, 58*:A3–A20.

INDEX